Flying Canucks II

Flying Canucks II
Pioneers *of* Canadian Aviation

PETER PIGOTT

HOUNSLOW
A member of the Dundurn Group

Contents

ACKNOWLEDGEMENTS

A s with all my books, I am indebted to several people. Every profession has men of intensity and spirit, and my greatest privilege in putting this book together was meeting or corresponding with Len Birchall, James Floyd, Bob Randall, and Claude I. Taylor. They patiently let me harass them for their memories and photographs. In researching *The Airman's Prayer*, an inquiry to the *London Free Press* newspaper showed that many in his hometown had not forgotten the author, " Bus" Davey. Bombardier, Air Canada and Canadian Airlines International allowed me to pillage their photo archives. A special vote of thanks to Shannon Ohama and Andrew Geider of Canadian, Brian Losito and Ross MacKenzie of Air Canada, Colin Fisher, Director of Public Relations, De Havilland Canada, and Garth Dingman of Canadair/Bombardier. Many thanks as well to Gwen Kerr, editor WCAM Magazine, Western Canada Aviation Museum, Winnipeg, Manitoba, for allowing me to use their article on Herb Seagrim.

In the course of writing this book, it became my good fortune to meet Fraser Muir, Ross Smyth, Jessie Bates of the Air Canada "Pionaires" and many Canadian Pacific Airlines retirees as well. I can unequivocally attest to their pride in being part of the great adventure of aviation.

To my family in Ottawa, Toronto and Montreal, all of whom have come to know when the madness is upon me to write ... may their patience and encouragement long continue.

Ottawa, 1997

INTRODUCTION

At any period in its history, a nation's mode of transportation assumes the hue of those who make it their own. Since 1908, Canada's transportation history has been happily coloured by the men who designed, built and flew aircraft in war and peace. The invention of the flying machine changed our country forever, giving its elusive vastness familiar form. Three years ago, in *Flying Canucks: Famous Canadian Aviators* I catalogued thirty-seven men and women who influenced our aeronautical culture. They were thumbnail sketches of early aviators, air aces, bush pilots and airline builders. This collection, while fewer in number, is more than sound bytes, especially of those personalities like C. D. Howe who cast a long shadow on our nation's history. Celebrity biographies have become the engines that drive our popular culture, so I have tried to stay away from mythologising Erroll Boyd, the first Canadian to fly the Atlantic Ocean or Len Birchall, the airman that Winston Churchill called "The Saviour of Ceylon." Instead, I have let their achievements speak for them. In some cases, just the name has become synonymous with their aircraft: Jim Floyd and the Avro Jetliner or "Buck" McNair's Spitfire over Malta.

All have been acknowledged for their accomplishments before — except for "Bus" Davey, an ordinary airman from London, Ontario, whose "Prayer" was deeply moving. He became for me, every one of the twelve thousand young men in the RCAF who, during the Second World War, gave their lives to fight Fascism. Wartime Canada's absolute czar, C.D. Howe used to say that running Trans-Canada Airlines was all he really wanted to do. He recognised that a national airline is a potent symbol of a country's fortunes, and from 1976 to 1993, Claude I. Taylor, guided Howe's child as if it were a work in progress.

Of the aviators chosen for this second book, who they are — or were — is not nearly as significant as what they stand for. Technologies evolve and national priorities change, but the qualities necessary to build aircraft, use them in war, and manage them in airlines, remain constant. All cultures are defined by their heroes, and this book traces the lives of eleven such Canadians, their steps into the unknown, their bravery and their contradictions. All in their own way, made a difference.

LEONARD BIRCHALL
THE SAVIOUR OF CEYLON

Soon after the end of the Second World War, Sir Winston Churchill and Canadian diplomat "Mike" Pearson were at a dinner at the British Embassy in Washington. In the glow of postwar victory, Churchill was asked if there ever was a moment when he thought that the war might have been lost. Was it after Dunkirk, or when Rommel was near Cairo, or perhaps at the fall of Singapore? While all those losses were bad, Churchill replied, it was the news that the Japanese fleet was approaching Ceylon that caused him the greatest despair. With Ceylon in enemy hands and Rommel in Egypt, the Axis could effectively gain control of the Indian Ocean and cut off Middle East oil supplies. In a typical Churchillian phrase, he said this would have "closed the ring"

S/L L.J. Birchall in the cockpit of a 413 Squadron Catalina.

around the Allies. It was only because an unknown Canadian airman, he continued, located the Japanese fleet and robbed it of the element of surprise, that the island colony was saved. It was just a pity the former prime minister added, that he had to pay for this heroism with his life, and would never know of his contribution to history.

Unable to contain himself any longer, Pearson broke in and said that the heroic Canadian airman had not only survived, but was at that very moment, stationed at the Canadian Embassy down the road. Churchill's surprise in hearing this must have only been equaled by the joy he felt knowing that Len Birchall was alive. "The Saviour of Ceylon" as he had called him had made "one of the most important individual contributions to victory."

Born in St. Catharine's, Ontario, Leonard Birchall was fascinated with airplanes as a child and took the familiar path to getting his pilot's licence. Through high school, he did odd-jobs at the local airfield to pay for flying lessons. After graduation in 1933, Birchall was accepted at the Royal Military College in Kingston that fall, a feat difficult enough at any time, but even more so during the Depression when the military accepted very, very few. He graduated four years later, and became a Provisional Flying Officer. He was stationed at the Flying Training School at the new RCAF base at Trenton, Ontario.

It was while getting his Pilot's Wings at Trenton that he began his long career with flying boats. Birchall trained on the venerable Vickers Vedettes that the RCAF were then using for aerial photography and forestry patrol. He began operational flying with No. 5 Bomber Reconnaissance Squadron formed at Dartmouth, Nova Scotia, late in 1938 for the Munich Crisis. This squadron was equipped with Stranraer flying boats which were a large twin engined biplane with canvas-covered wings and bags of flying wire. The RCAF used the "Stranny" or "Whistling Birdcage" in a multitude of roles from passenger and freight carrying to anti-submarine patrols. As a junior officer Birchall performed all the mundane jobs that came the way of junior officers like chauffeuring VIPs on inspection tours.

When the Second World War began, Birchall was a Flight Lieutenant and Signals Specialist with Number 5 Squadron flying coastal patrols out of Dartmouth. In May 1940, when a declaration of war with Italy seemed imminent, he was ordered to locate Italian merchant ships still on the St. Lawrence River. The Canadian government hoped to capture the ships and intern the crews before they could escape into the Atlantic.

On June 1, 1940, Birchall found the Italian freighter the *Capo Lena* off Anticosti Island. It was making a dash for the open sea before a declaration of war could be announced over the radio. Birchall shadowed the ship all day waiting for the hostilities to begin so that he could swoop down on it. But by dusk when there was still no word, he was forced to return to base. The next morning he took off and found the ship again, in the Gulf of the St. Lawrence and very close to the high seas. He continued to follow it all day, but once more, there was no declaration, and at nightfall, the RCAF patrol reluctantly flew home, allowing the Capo Lena to disappear into the Atlantic.

Finally on June 10, 1940, Italy declared war on Canada, and Birchall took off once more looking for other Italian ships that might still be on the St. Lawrence. One, the *Capo Nola* had just left Quebec City, and was making a run for the Gulf and the Atlantic. It's crew must have watched incredulously as the Stranraer, like a dowager aunt pretending to be a fighter aircraft, bore down on them with about as much menace as the biplane could manage. The Italian captain however, was sufficiently frightened by the pilot's intent, and ran his vessel aground on the nearest

It was in a No. 5 (BR) Squadron Stranraer that Birchall hunted down and captured the Italian ship on June 10, 1940, in the St. Lawrence.

sand bank, and then tried to set fire to it. Birchall set the Stranraer down nearby ready to claim the ship as a prize just as a Royal Canadian naval vessel showed up. The *Capo Nola* crew became the first Italian prisoners-of-war for Canada. It was also Birchall's first taste of action.

The start of the Second World War found the aerial defence of Halifax woefully inadequate. There was no torpedo-bomber force available, and although No. 5 was designated as a maritime patrol squadron, it had no depth charges to protect the shipping in the harbour from marauding U-boats. The air force even flew some ancient Westland Wapitis down to Halifax as a stop-gap measure. These biplanes had been used by the British during the 1920s in the Middle East, and the RCAF were able to snap them up at a bargain prices. The Canadians used to swear that the Wapitis still reeked of camel dung and called them "What-a-pities". Birchall noted that when the Wapitis arrived, base personnel immediately took the wings off them. As he later explained, presumably this was because had they been used, the remainder of the air force would have done nothing but search and rescue missions looking for them.

The only other RCAF aircraft in the vicinity were a few Northrop Deltas. These were sturdy, low wing monoplanes on floats, known for the noisiness of their single, large engines.[1] The other problem they had was that on take-off, a vacuum would form just behind the step and hold the float down. You had to rush up and down the harbour, trying to build up enough speed to combat the negative lift caused by the vacuum. It was a noisy, frustrating aircraft to get off the water.

Birchall recalled that he and Jack Twigg, a friend from Royal Military College days were once trying to get up enough speed to take off in a Delta. They roared up and down the harbour with Twigg getting angrier and angrier each time the suction of the float would hold them down. Finally, Twigg decided that they were either going to take off or go charging up on shore. At the last minute he began to bounce the Delta, getting more and more speed with each bounce and then suddenly they were airborne! But only just. A head of them some trees and a hill loomed up — and the closer they got they saw there was a very large building on that hill. They cleared the roof of the building at, as Birchall said by "zilch feet", breaking he was sure, half its windows with the noise.

---

1 Like the Harvard, another notoriously noisy aircraft, this was due to the Delta's propellor tips going "supersonic."

They both knew that the building was a convent and turned back to the harbour to land and apologize. The fliers drove up to the convent, on the way rehearsing the story that they had been on a vital war mission. Once there they asked to see the Mother Superior. She graciously invited them in and they presented their case. One of their aircraft they explained, *might* have on take off, come quite close to the roof of the her convent. They hoped that no one had been upset, but as there could be U-boats out there, the aircraft's courageous crew were risking their lives trying to find them.

The Mother Superior told them not to worry as this was really a hospital and the delivery room was on the top floor. By skimming over it, they had no idea how much help they had given the poor girls!

In 1941, Birchall was promoted to Squadron Leader and became Chief Navigational Officer at Number 2 Training Command, Winnipeg. By the time the Japanese attacked Pearl Harbour in December, he was in Bermuda flying aircraft for the Trans-Atlantic Ferry Command. Then at Christmas, Birchall was posted to Scotland to become second in command of 413 Squadron RCAF then in the Shetland Islands. To maintain a Canadian presence in the battle against the U-Boats, Ottawa

Canadians in 413 Squadron, 17 March 1941. Birchall is in the back row, fifth from the right.

PL-7403

Leonard Birchall **17**

had decided to send an RCAF maritime squadron to the North Sea. Great pains were taken to keep the squadron's officers and crew Canadian. Equipped with Consolidated Catalinas, a vast improvement on the old Stranraers, 413 was charged with providing protection for convoys going to the Soviet Union. The "Cats" were slow, cumbersome flying boats, but they had been designed for long-range patrols and had a twenty-five hour endurance. This enabled them to escort a convoy for about 600 miles from their base (compared with the 440 miles of the Sunderland and 250 miles of the Hudson — the other Coastal Command aircraft). But while it was undoubtedly the best maritime patrol aircraft of its day, the Catalina was unamoured and lightly armed. If it encountered Luftwaffe fighters, it stood no chance of survival.

In October, 1941, 413 was moved to Sullom Voe in the Shetland Islands to begin anti-submarine patrols over convoys bound for Murmansk. It was commanded by Wing Commander R.G. Briese, a popular pre-war RCAF officer who had experience in maritime patrol at Patricia Bay, British Columbia. However, the fury of the Shetlands storms must have been a far cry from anything that he had ever encountered on the West coast. Their Catalinas designed like it's name in the sunny climes of California, were unheated and ill-suited for the bitter North Sea cold. Unlike the larger Sunderlands, they rolled heavily in the high waves at Sullom Voe. The patrols were performed in the worst, coldest weather that their crew had ever experienced. On 22 October, the squadron was ordered to provide an aircraft to fly up the Norwegian coast on a photo-reconnaissance mission. The British were afraid that the German battleships *Scharnhorst* and *Gneisenau* were hiding in the fjords, and that they might be unleashed on to the Russian convoys. Everyone knew that flying over Norway would put the aircraft within range of Luftwaffe fighters. It was a suicide mission as Briese was well aware. Rather than condemn any of his crews to certain death, the C.O. took the flight himself. He and his crew were never seen again.

The bad weather that followed Briese's loss brought morale even lower. The blizzards and squalls that winter prevented much flying from taking place and on 11 November, in a severe storm, four of the Catalinas were sunk at their moorings by huge waves. The loss of morale among the Canadian personnel (and their anger at headquarters for ordering such a mission) was the welcome that Birchall as the squadron's number two had to deal with.

The new commanding officer was Birchall's old colleague, Jack Twigg. He was also ordered to have the squadron send out a photo-reconnaissance Catalina to Norway, this time to photograph a possible Luftwaffe night-fighter base near Trondheim. Like the one before, the mission as both Twigg and Birchall knew, was completely suicidal. Not only was the Catalina useless against fighters, but in order to take photos at night, a flare had to be first dropped over the target which would give the aircraft's location away. Contrary to all airforce regulations, Twigg and Birchall volunteered to fly the mission themselves. They were so sure of not returning that they chose only a radio operator as their crew to report on the Luftwaffe base location.

The trio took off from Sullom Voe into the turbulent winter weather that only added to the danger ... or so it seemed. The storm developed into a white-out blizzard over Norway which made finding the airfield impossible. With the visibility at zero, their camera could not take photographs of the airfield. Fortunately, the swirling snow also prevented the Luftwaffe's fighters from taking off; it was this that allowed Twigg and Birchall to escape with their lives. They had escaped certain death because of the weather.

Events on the other side of the world changed Birchall's life forever. By early 1942, the Japanese had conquered most of the Pacific and the European colonies in the Far East. The American fleet at Pearl Harbour was still out of action. Hong Kong and Singapore had fallen, and the Dutch East Indies were under attack. The far-ranging Japanese fleets seemed invincible and both Australia and New Zealand looked like they might be isolated. To defend themselves against the surprise attacks by carrier-borne fighters and bombers, the British bases in Ceylon (now Sri Lanka) urgently needed maritime reconnaissance patrols over the Indian Ocean. The reason for this was that there was no radar on Ceylon; the only way to get a warning of a carrier-borne raid was by maritime patrol aircraft. The RCAF's 413 Squadron was ordered to the RAF flying boat base at Koggalla near Galle. Ottawa was less than pleased with the 413 move to Ceylon as it meant that the RCAF squadron would be under complete British control.

While the rest of the personnel would travel by troopship, the Catalinas were flown out in pairs by their crews. In a journey that would have made headlines at home before the war, Squadron Leader Birchall flew from Scotland with a stopover in Gibraltar, over the Mediterranean, and landed on the Nile near Cairo. From Egypt they continued to the Persian Gulf before setting down at Korangi Creek near Karachi in present day Pakistan. Here the second Catalina developed engine trouble and Birchall and his crew flew on alone down the Indian coast to Ceylon. Koggalla was on a small lake; at that time home to an RAF flying boat squadron recently reinforced by Dutch Catalina crews who had escaped from the East Indies when Java surrendered on 8 March.

The demoralized British Army in Burma was then in full retreat from the Japanese. Rangoon fell on 9 March and the Indian ports of Calcutta and Madras were suddenly on the front-line. All shipping in the Bay of Bengal was now threatened. The sleepy island of Ceylon suddenly assumed critical importance as the key to control of the Indian Ocean. Its few defences were hastily reinforced with whatever the Allies could spare from campaigns in North Africa, the Pacific and China. Serious military strategists knew that it could never hold out against a Japanese invasion. Crowded with refugees from Singapore, Ceylon nervously awaited the inevitable.

To keep an army supplied in the Burmese jungles was a logistical nightmare — as the Japanese discovered. There was not even a railway line between Burma and Siam. Tokyo thus gave Admiral Chuichi Nagumo, the victor of Pearl Harbour, the task of protecting the sea lanes to the Imperial Army in Burma. Nagumo's only opposition in the Indian Ocean was a small British fleet under Admiral Sir James Somerville. Somerville had a collection of World War I battleships and one small aircraft carrier, all that could be spared from the ferocious campaigns taking place in the Atlantic and Mediterranean. The problem was Somerville did not know where the Japanese invasion fleet was. He counted on the long range Catalinas flying boats to be his eyes for the defence of Ceylon — or in future terminology — an early warning system.

In the dawn of 4 April, barely a day after he had arrived, Birchall and his crew were ordered to patrol south of the island. The patrol was to cover an area about 350 miles south-east of Ceylon, sufficient to warn of an enemy dawn raid. Had they been at Koggalla long, the Canadian crew would have discovered that this was a suicide mission. It was common knowledge around the base — and indeed the island — that the Japanese carriers were out there waiting for the signal to launch the invasion. The crew of a Dutch Catalina who had seen the Japanese in action flatly refused the same mission. Had they known, 413's personnel would have seen it as a repeat of the Norwegian patrol that Briese had carried out. The Canadians were ordered to stay aloft for twenty-four hours, returning to Koggalla Lake at dawn the next day.

Twelve hours of patrolling saw Birchall 350 miles from Ceylon beginning his flight home. His navigator asked for one more patrol while he took a celestial fix. At that moment, someone saw specks on the horizon. It had to be the invasion fleet. As the radio operator sent out a report, the Catalina ponderously headed into the centre of the rows of ships. Colombo needed to know the type and number, their speed and position. The crew counted out four battleships and five aircraft carriers, the latter with fighters spilling off their flat tops, angrily making for the flying boat. Because they had been flying at 2,000 feet they had come in under the shield of patrolling Zeros

The Zeros pounced on the Catalina, their pilots realising that if they could prevent the radio message from taking place, the surprise attack on Somerville's ships would be complete.[2] The first shells slammed into the radio compartment, injuring the operator. They could not be sure that the message had been received as Colombo had not acknowledged it. Tracer bullets set the upper gasoline tank on fire and the interior of the aircraft was filled with smoke, wounded men and sloshing gasoline. Birchall put the Catalina into a desperate dive to escape the Zeros. The crew put the fire out twice, but the third time the gasoline, the ammunition and the pyrotechnics started to explode; there was no hope of containing the blaze. As the flying boat hit the water with a thud, Birchall's crew put the two wounded into Mae Wests, threw them into the water, jumping in after them.

The Zeros continued to strafe the burning Catalina as the bleeding men swam away from it. In their fury, the Japanese turned their attention to the two wounded men, floating helplessly in their life jackets. Cannon fire tore into the pair smashing them into a pulp. The six remaining crew dived underwater to escape the same fate, knowing that their bloody wounds were sure to attract sharks very soon. Then a Japanese destroyer picked them up.

With three airmen very badly wounded and three not too badly off, the Canadians were lined up on deck and the interrogation began. The

2   The Japanese did not know that, rather than risk his fleet which was inferior to theirs, within the harbour, the British admiral had dispersed his ships to a secret naval base at Addu Atoll, south west of Ceylon.

Japanese desperately needed to know if the radio warning had been sent. In perfect English a Japanese officer asked who the senior officer was and when Birchall identified himself, the beatings began. He denied sending any message and just as they had the Japanese convinced, Colombo came on the air and asked for a repeat of their last message.

Although the element of surprise was lost, Nagumo launched an air attack on Colombo on 5 April. Warned by Birchall, the RAF was able to scramble forty-two Hurricanes to meet them — eight of which were flown by Canadians. Although only twenty-three of his Zeros were shot down, it was a loss that Nagumo operating far from home could ill afford. He knew that within a month his carriers would be needed to provide air cover for a Japanese invasion of Port Moresby in New Guinea. Somerville's fleet had escaped; while the major harbours and naval bases at Colombo would be repeatedly bombed, the invasion never took place.

Four days later the RCAF's only other Catalina at Koggalla flown by Flight Lieutenant R. Thomas sighted the same enemy fleet approaching the Indian port of Trincomalee. This time the Canadians were not as fortunate. When Thomas's "Cat" was inevitably shot down, there were no survivors. Admiral Somerville, alerted to the Japanese strategy, managed to blunt the attack, with the loss of his two cruisers and aircraft carrier. The RCAF Catalinas gradually arrived in Ceylon over the next few days but the squadron was not complete until a troopship brought the ground crew in late May.

By then the Japanese had turned back from the Indian Ocean and a month later, the same fleet that had been bloodied by Somerville was wiped out in the Battle of Midway. It would prove to be the beginning of the end for the Axis.

But Birchall and his crew were to know none of this. They endured the anger of their captors spending the first days of captivity locked in the ship's paint locker. They were later moved later to the Flagship which was an aircraft carrier. Disembarked in Japan, the Canadians were sent to a POW camp in Yokohama. In it and subsequent camps around the city, they endured three years of slave labour, starvation and sadistic beatings. As the senior officer in the camp, Birchall defied the commander at peril to his own life. He intervened on behalf of his men, knowing that he would receive brutal punishment for doing so. After once breaking a guard's jaw, he was put into solitary confinement and given a month of hard labour. This did not deter him — while working at a shipyard he organised a sit-down strike at the camp. As punishment he was sent to a special disciplinary camp for difficult POWs. Throughout the years he had all the atrocities recorded, and at the war crimes trial in 1947, the contents of these diaries were used to convict several of the guards.

For his heroism in warning of the Japanese fleet, Squadron Leader Len Birchall was awarded the Distinguished Flying Cross, but it was for his leadership and courage while in the prison camp that he was given the Order of the British Empire for Gallantry. He came back to Ottawa in 1945 as a Wing Commander, and two years later, was appointed Assistant Air Attaché, Canadian Joint Staff, Washington D.C. In 1950 he returned to Canada and became the Commanding Officer of the RCAF Station at Goose Bay, and in 1958, the C.O. of RCAF Station, North Bay. Birchall's career took a diplomatic turn when he became Air Commodore, External Affairs Chief Administrator at NATO in 1963. He returned to the Royal Military Academy that year as its Commandant and, as such was an Honourary Aide-de-Camp to their Excellencies, Governor General Vanier and Michener. Although he retired from the RCAF in 1968, he remained the Honourary Colonel of 413 Squadron — the same one he flew Catalinas in 1941.

He returned to Ceylon (now Sri Lanka) in 1967 and in 1992, to celebrate the fiftieth anniversary of his being shot down. In 1995 he went back once more to dedicate a memorial at Koggalla in honour of all the 413 Squadron members who died there during the war. On April 21, 1996, Leonard Birchall celebrated sixty-two years in the service, the first ever to do so. As he says: "only Her Majesty, The Queen Mother will be able to equal that record in 1997." Those fortunate enough to hear him talk about his career, know he is an entertaining speaker, completely self-effacing about his courage that early morning over the Indian Ocean. But for most Canadians, he will always be in Churchill's phrase, " The Saviour of Ceylon."

ERROLL BOYD
THE FIRST CANADIAN TO FLY THE ATLANTIC

If asked to name the earliest Trans-Atlantic fliers, most Canadians could come up with Charles Lindbergh and possibly Alcock and Brown. If asked to name the first Canadian to fly the Atlantic, how many could identify Erroll Boyd? Yet three years after Lindbergh's flight, Boyd was not only the first Canadian to complete the ocean crossing, but unlike Lindbergh and Alcock and Brown, he did it in the autumn when the weather is poor and the daylight hours shorter. Given that he had little financial backing and his aircraft had been well-used before in another record flight only adds credit to his epic accomplishment.

Erroll Boyd was born in Toronto in 1892 into an affluent family. His father was a senior executive with the insurance company Confederation Life and could trace his lineage to Lord Erroll of Scotland. Young Boyd attended prestigious St. Andrew's College — by coincidence the alma mater of aviation pioneer J.A.D. McCurdy. If the Boyds hoped that their son would follow in his father's footsteps and enter a comfortable career in insurance this was probably dashed the day an aviator called Lincoln Beachey came to Canada. "Link" as the media dubbed him was as the aviation historian Frank Ellis would write: " a born airman ... The first to perform loop-the-loops, inverted flying, spins and dives, he was the envy of every man and boy in North America."[1] Teenaged Erroll was very fortunate to fly as a passenger with Beachey in his specially strengthened Curtiss hydroplane. Although he did not know, this ride would be Boyd's first step to the crossing of the Atlantic two decades later.

---

1   Ellis, Frank. *Canada's Flying Heritage* Toronto: University of Toronto Press, 1954. On March 14, 1915, while performing over San Francisco Bay, the wings of Beachey's machine could no longer take the strain. They collapsed and he plunged into the water, and died by drowning.

But at that time an Atlantic flight was probably the furthest thing from the young man's mind. World War I had broken out and as there was no Canadian air force to enlist in, Boyd joined the Queen's Own Rifles and went to England. Once there, he tried to join the Royal Flying Corps. He was turned down because of colour-blindness but was accepted as an officer in the Royal Naval Air Service which had much less stringent entrance standards. It took the authority of the Canadian High Commissioner in London Sir George Perley to get Boyd his transfer and commission.

He was taught to fly by none other than John Alcock who with Arthur Whitton Brown would become the first to fly the Atlantic four years later. We can only speculate as to what the two might have discussed. Boyd trained on several types of aircraft, the most memorable being a Wright biplane which had wing warping rather than aerlerons for lateral control. However he did manage to solo in a Short pusher, and by 1915 was flying operationally in a home defence squadron.

In response to the Royal Navy's blockade of Germany, the Kaiser authorised the use of Zeppelins to bomb Britain. The dirigibles flew high above the English countryside, usually at night and at first were out of range of the anti-aircraft batteries below. More a nuisance than of strategic value, the sausage shapes of the Zeppelins made them a highly visible symbol of German aggression, and outraged the British public. In response to the threat, home defence fighter squadrons ringed London to shoot them down. The procedure was to get above the dirigible if possible and drop twenty pound bombs onto its mass. It was a futile exercise, as Boyd discovered, used more for the propaganda value. All a Zeppelin had to do to escape a British fighter was shed its ballast and shoot up out of range. It would not be until September 1916 with improved aero engines and searchlights that the defenders would gain the upper hand. By then, Erroll Boyd was out of action. In 1915, his squadron was sent to Dunkirk. The French airfield was within range of the German seaplane base at Zeebrugge in Belgium. In a bombing mission of the seaplane sheds, Boyd was shot down but fortunately was able to make it across the border into neutral Holland. He would be interned and later released to the Allies.

While on leave in New York in 1917 Boyd married the musical dancer Evelyn Carberry whom he had first met when she played the Royal Alexandria Theatre in Toronto. The newly-weds plunged into the jazz scene as Al Jolson threw them a party and Boyd even wrote the lyrics to a war tune *For Love of Liberty*. To earn a living, he became a test pilot for the Curtiss aircraft company in Buffalo. It was a suicidal profession that Boyd only just survived. In 1917, he was almost killed testing a new all-metal aircraft called a Lanzius I over Long Island.

He returned to Toronto at the end of the war and got a job running a car rental fleet at the York garage on Bloor Street. For him and hundreds of other pilots, there seemed no future in aviation. The world had a surplus of pilots and aircraft and the public did not want to be reminded of anything associated with the carnage of the war. With a growing family, Boyd bided his time renting out Model T Fords for $1.00 an hour.

But it was the decade of the Roaring Twenties and hoping to restart his musical career, he moved back to New York. One of his songs *Dreams* became a Broadway hit but in 1924, when his daughter Jean fell out of the apartment window to her death, he gave it up and left New York. He worked as a manager for the British food company Crosse & Blackwell in 1926 at their Detroit office, doing well enough to buy a Stinson biplane. When Charles Lindbergh flew to Paris the following year all North America caught aviation fever. Boyd who had always wanted to fly the Atlantic himself immediately tried to get commercial sponsorship for a non-stop flight as far as Moscow. When this failed he returned to Canada and worked briefly flying the mail run between Montreal and Rimouski.

The winter of 1928 found him flying in Mexico and it was here that he learned to fly by instruments. Called blind flying then — it was a skill that would prove valuable two years later when he was crossing the Atlantic. Most pilots at that time flew by the seat of their pants — i.e. visually — from landmark to landmark. The company was based on the Yucatan peninsula and given the local climate and geography, this was approach impossible. Boyd enjoyed the adventure but the rough country was unsuited to raising a family and in 1929, the Boyds left Mexico for New York. There he joined Coastal Airways, an airline that flew amphibian-seaplanes between New York and Albany.

When the stock market crash bankrupted the airline that year, Boyd landed a well paid job flying for Charles Levine. A former scrap dealer who became a millionaire, Levine was a colourful character who enjoyed the publicity of hanging out with pilots. In 1926, he bought an aviation company and among its assets was a Bellanca WB-2. A sturdy high wing monoplane — its steel tube fuselage was covered with fabric and the engine was fuel-efficient 220 hp. Wright J-5. Naming it the *Columbia,* Levine seems to have made it available to pilots who wanted to emulate Lindbergh by making record-breaking flights. Two weeks after Lindbergh's crossing, Clarence Chamberlain flew non-stop from New York to Germany in the *Columbia* with Levine as a passenger. In 1928 the same aircraft was used by Wilbur Stultz to break another record by flying non-stop from New York to Havana.

As early as 1916 Boyd had told the press of his dream to fly the Atlantic; it was not until 1930 that he was able to achieve part of it. Using the Bellanca, he and an experienced pilot Roger Q. Williams planned to fly from New York to Bermuda and back. There was no airport in Bermuda then and the object was to demonstrate the commercial feasibility of an air mail drop. As they were venturing out into the Atlantic, Boyd chose Harry Connor as a navigator. Connor had been trained by the United States Navy. This proved a wise move because throughout the seventeen hour flight visibility was poor and Connor's navigational skills probably saved their lives. The Canadian knew the *Columbia* well now and was impressed with Harry Connor's skills. A trans-Atlantic crossing was becoming more feasible.

But the effects of the Depression on businesses was being felt and Levine's was not immune. One night, his hangar filled with aircraft burnt down under suspicious circumstances — insurance investigators found that all the instruments had been removed from the charred aircraft. On hearing about the fire, Boyd was afraid that the *Columbia* was part of the tangled remains.

Fortuitously, without informing him, Roger Q. Williams had flown the aircraft across the border to Montreal and stored it at St. Hubert Airport. Relieved that the *Columbia* was safe in Canada and that Levine was too preoccupied with business to interfere, Boyd set about raising capital to finance his trans-Atlantic venture.

Prohibition was still in force in the United States, and Jack O'Brien, a New York speak easy owner was hired to drum up business. Together they raised some money and even signed a contract with Hearst Publications for the exclusive rights to the story of the flight. Then they took a train to Montreal where the aircraft was being stored. To raise more money, Boyd had the American flag expediently painted over on the aircraft's rudder and the *Columbia* re christened the *Maple Leaf.* Then

The *Columbia*, renamed *Maple Leaf* on the beach at Tresco, Scilly Isles, October 10-11, 1930.

they flew to Toronto to appeal to the patriotic and adventuresome spirit of potential investors. But because of the Depression, there was little money to spare and he returned to Montreal empty-handed.

When they returned to St. Hubert Airport, they found the RCMP waiting for them. Roger Q. Williams claimed that Levine owed him back pay and that until it was paid, the *Columbia* (as he knew it) was his. Simultaneously, his Bermuda trip navigator Harry Connor flew into Montreal lobbying to go on the flight. Connor also warned that with the lateness of the season, the good flying weather required to cross the ocean was coming to an end. The navigator did bring with him a Sperry artificial horizon that had already been tested by Jimmy Doolittle. But it was his expensive new tweed suit, that he wore with bowtie, hat, cane and gloves that really impressed the broke and rumpled Boyd and O'Brien. When asked where he had got it, Connor casually said that he had visited the men's shop in the hotel lobby and charged it to Boyd's account!

With the advent of fall, both the flying season and Boyd's finances were slipping away but he still had a great capacity to make friends.

Thomas Coonan, a King's Counsel offered to plead the legal case to get ownership of the *Maple Leaf* without a fee; after three weeks of negotiations, the aircraft was released into Boyd's custody. Then the local manager of Canada Dry Ginger Ale donated the money to pay for their fuel as far as Newfoundland. An example of Boyd's desperation was that they had to sneak out of the hotel without paying. Here too, friends helped — in a way. A group of McGill students with a waiter's help smuggled them down by the service elevator, through the kitchen, into the alley and drove them to the airport. After he paid the hanger dues owing on the *Maple Leaf* Boyd had exactly $18.00 left ... hardly enough for fuel from Newfoundland onward. A hat was passed around the spectators and it is said that even the local RCMP constable guarding the aircraft contributed some money.

On 13 September, 1930, the *Maple Leaf* lifted off from St. Hubert's rough-surfaced runway for Newfoundland in light rain and overcast conditions. By the time Boyd and Connor were over Cape Breton, darkness was closing fast and with stormy weather visible, they put down at Charlottetown, Prince Edward Island. The airport was part of the farm of the family of Colonel Jack Jenkins D.S.O. — an aviation-mad family. His wife Louise Jenkins would later become the first woman to get her pilot's licence in the province. Grounded by the weather for ten days, Boyd and Connor stayed with the Jenkins family.

Then on 24 September they took off and made it to Harbour Grace airfield, Newfoundland. Harbour Grace was the traditional jumping-off point for trans-Atlantic fliers. Between 1927-36 aviation legends like Kingsford Smith, Wiley Post, Amelia Earhart and James Mollison had all used the narrow runway. But once more the weather was bad and they were delayed for a further two weeks. Anxiously they waited on continual updates of conditions over the Atlantic and the Canadian Meteorological Service in Toronto did their best in co-operate. Boyd and Connor even arranged for ships at sea to radio the weather conditions via New York, tracking them in both directions to get a better overall picture.

Connor would later say that with easterly winds and gales blowing over the entire Atlantic for nearly three weeks there seemed to be no let up, and he and Boyd were becoming quite disheartened. Then on 8 October they received the following report from the Toronto meteorological office: "Area of high pressure over Newfoundland extends eastward over the Atlantic to about longitude 30 degrees (this was the halfway point of the flight). Conditions over the eastern Atlantic and British Isles too stormy to start today." Even with that warning, Boyd and Connor calculated that this was probably the best they could hope for at this time of year, and decided to risk it the next day. A take-off at sunrise would give them as much of the daylight hours as possible. The Toronto office advised them to wait as there was nothing further to add to the dismal circumstances.

Harbour Grace was covered by heavy fog on 9 October and Boyd had to delay taking off until it lifted in the afternoon. This was a disappointment as he had hoped that an earlier start would have allowed them to use up at least 100 gallons of fuel before nightfall and lightened the *Maple Leaf* by 600 pounds. With a heavy fuel load, he knew from his Bermuda flight that the aircraft tended to drift off on either wing which would have sent them plunging into the Atlantic. As Lindbergh had found out, getting a perfect fuel/weight balance was crucial. The *Maple Leaf* carried a total of 460 US gallons on take off, giving it thirty-five hours flying time. With the combined weight of the crew and fifteen pounds of official mail, this gave it a gross weight of 5,200 pounds. Thus a radio set couldn't be carried because its weight of eighty pounds represented thirteen gallons of fuel or one hour of flying time.

At 16:18 Greenwich Mean Time, with a light easterly wind at their tail, Boyd and Connor lifted from Harbour Grace. Getting a heavily burdened aircraft airborne off a runway about 3,000 feet in length, required all a pilot's skill and both breathed easier as it lifted over the rocks at the water's edge. Before he left, Boyd said that he had been waiting for this opportunity for many years and that it was not a hit or miss idea.

The flight plan called for them to fly the great circle route to Swansea in Wales, then Bristol, and finally land at Croydon. An hour and thirty-five minutes after takeoff, the freighter *Quaker City* spotted them flying eastward 200 feet above the waves, 100 miles east-northeast of Cape Race, the eastern tip of Newfoundland. That afternoon they made a ground speed of sixty-eight mph, and by sunset this had increased to seventy mph. To check their position with the stars, Connor had to climb over the main fuel tank and hold a sextant out of the observation hatch. The earth inductor compass had been rendered useless because of the heavy vibration at takeoff and they had to rely on the two magnetic compasses.

The Cunard liner *Lancastria* saw them go over at 22:40 Zulu; Boyd signaled her by flashlight, spelling out strangely enough *Columbia* not *Maple Leaf* to it in Morse. Because of the darkness, the Sperry artificial horizon proved invaluable. Boyd would later say that it was like piloting a car in coal mine. With dead reckoning navigation they calculated that by 03:30Z they had arrived at 35 degrees west longitude and the halfway point had been passed. At that point they changed to a northward course to follow the shipping lane.

As they climbed through the cloud, Boyd saw that the thermometer registered below freezing. Then the black strip he had painted on the leading edge of the wing began to be covered with ice. Before the days of de-icing boots on wings, pilots had a healthy fear of ice buildup on their wings as it increased drag and changed the shape of the airfoil. Boyd quickly descended, turning south to a warmer temperature.

They came out of the cloud at 12,000 feet, happy to see the moon. The weather continued to be rough throughout the night and since Connor was not a pilot, Boyd flew alone. Whenever he began to doze off, his navigator held a sponge soaked in water to the back of his neck. Ten and a half hours after flying in the darkness, glimmers of dawn appeared and by 9:40 Connor was able to take a reading. He put them at 47 degrees north, 18 degrees west and heading for the Bay of Biscay. Boyd then turned 25 degrees left towards Land's End. The end seemed very close.

Then they discovered because of a clogged fuel line, the 100 gallons of fuel in the reserve tank would not pump up into the gravity tank of the right wing. The loss of this reserve meant that Boyd had to reduce his airspeed by throttling back and rely on the southwesterly winds to push them towards Britain.

They saw the coast of the Scilly Isles at 16:02 Z off the port bow and Connor plotted a course for Plymouth. As there was no airfield on the Scilly Isle, they had to risk the twenty-three miles that separated them from England. Boyd didn't want to take the chance, having come so far, of being forced to ditch in the sea and decided to make for the Isles. Tresco the largest of the two was two miles long and a mile wide and Boyd aimed the *Maple Leaf* at a sloping beach. As a precaution against fire if they did crash, the 100 gallons of fuel was released from the reserve tank and Connor crawled to the rear of the plane to give it a better center of gravity. To make matters worse, both airmen saw that it was high tide and that the usable portion of the beach was lessening with each second. With a few gallons of fuel left and little more than 200 feet to use, Boyd set the aircraft down on the soft sand. It came to a halt a few inches from the lapping waves. He had become the first Canadian to fly the Atlantic Ocean.

There was considerable excitement in the small community. Workers from a nearby bulb farm helped drag the *Maple Leaf* to higher ground, and the governor of the islands, Major A.A. Dorrien-Smith, did not ask that the two airmen stay with him for the night, but arranged that aviation fuel be brought over by seaplane from the Air Force Station at Mountbatten, Plymouth.

At low tide at 13:02Z the next afternoon, Boyd and Connor took off from the beach at Tresco, arriving at Croydon three hours later on 11 October, 1930 at 15:55. Among the huge crowd that greeted them was the ubiquitous Charles Levine. In London Boyd and Conner were feted by Canadian Prime Minister R.B. Bennett who was attending the Imperial Conference and, although the disaster of the R-101 airship had taken place a few days before they arrived, even the Prince of Wales received them. Among the many congratulatory telegrams was one from the acting Prime Minister in Ottawa, Sir George Perley. Boyd telephoned his family including his parents from London. His mother told reporters in Toronto that her son was used to overcoming obstacles. As a four year old he used to dive off steamers at Muskoka!

Although he met movie stars and royalty, the best thing to happen to Boyd in London occured when a wealthy Canadian, Sherwin Cottingham, bought the *Maple Leaf* for him from Levine. Boyd and Connor flew on to celebrations in Amsterdam, Berlin and Paris, returning to even greater receptions in Montreal and Toronto. Sadly, the faithful Bellanca was lost in a hanger fire in 1934. Boyd himself went through a penurious time until *Toronto Star* reporter, Gregory Clark hearing of it, convinced his newspaper to hire the first Canadian to fly the Atlantic. Erroll Boyd became the aviation editor of the *Star Weekly* and in 1938 organised the Aviation Scouts of Canada.[2] During the Second World War, like Billy Bishop, he helped recruit neutral American

2   I am indebted to aviation author Ross Smyth for most of the information on Erroll Boyd. As a boy, Smyth was a member of the Aviation Scouts and had met Boyd in 1938 when he won an airline flight from Buffalo to Miami. Smyth who went on to become one of TCA's first trans-Atlantic flight dispatchers, never forgot Canada's Lindbergh.

pilots for service in the Royal Air Force and civilian trans-Atlantic ferrying. In 1957 he suffered a stroke and he died three years later.

Erroll Boyd personified the aviation pioneer who was even then a rarity in the profession. With the 1930s, aviation was becoming too expensive (and too complicated) for a single individual to play a crucial part in. Lindbergh had been backed by businessmen from the city of St. Louis, but in Depression-racked Canada Boyd could not raise enough financing. The first Canadian to fly the Atlantic (in the perilous autumn months too,) spent crucial years scrambling for financial support. Unknown to most of his countrymen, his courage has never been fully recognised.

"BUS" DAVEY
THE AIRMAN'S PRAYER

Courage comes in many forms and "Bus" Davey would have been embarrassed to be thought courageous. During the Second World War, alone among all the major Allied countries, Canada was never threatened. Yet this ordinary Canadian airman doing his duty far from home, allowed his young life to be cut violently short in defence of it.

Ernest Raymond Davey was born on November 25, 1921, in London, Ontario. His father George Davey, together with thousands of British immigrants, immediately joined the Army when the First World War began. He had been working on a ship on the Great Lakes for two years and as soon as it docked at Goderich, several of the crew left the boat and took the train to London, Ontario to join up. The imperial bonds were very strong — the Mother Country was in trouble and George like most young men was swept up in the patriotic fervour of the hour. It wasn't if you were going to join up, but which outfit that men asked each other. War was an adventure and, George like many of his generation, must have been raised on stories of the Crimean and Boer wars. Or it could have been that the Army provided the unemployed immigrant with three square meals a day, uniforms and travel.

The London 1st Battalion was sent overseas with the 1st Division and George was thrown into the Battle of Ypres in April 1915. Whatever illusions he had about the glamour of war must have been shattered in the mud of the trenches with the carnage and brutality of no mans land. A German bullet hit George in the chest and, the wound was so critical, that he was not expected to live. However, he recovered sufficiently to be hospitalised in England. While convalescing in Wales, George met Selina and married her. He took her back to London, Ontario to begin a family and they settled in a house at 13 Southgate Street in south London.

"Bus" got his wings in February 1943, and was posted overseas. Before he left home, he wrote *An Airman's Prayer*.

George got a job at Westminister Hospital, a veteran's institution. It was a close-knit, typically middle class neighbourhood. On the other side of their backyard lived the Giles family, the father Harry, an X-Ray technician, was also employed at the hospital.

The brashness of the Jazz Age soon submerged the horrors of the war and Canada changed almost overnight. There were electric lights, movies and movie stars (albeit silent). Gramophones brought music into homes and Ford Model Ts became more frequent than horse-drawn carriages on London's streets. At the annual agricultural fair, the hot-air balloons gave way to biplanes, their pilots (usually Royal Flying Corp veterans) earning a precarious living charging for rides or carrying barnstorming acrobats. Everyone from the prime minister down knew that there would never be another war, the League of Nations would see to that. The Great War that George had survived would go down in history as the " War to end all Wars."

Ernest was the second of five children — and, for reasons unkown, was nicknamed "Bus". He was remembered as a normal kid who had average school grades at Tecumseh school and earned his allowance delivering newspapers. He loved to tease his three sisters and was idolised by his younger brother. On his tenth birthday, "Bus" was given a German shepherd dog he named Jerry, who followed him everywhere. The prosperous Twenties had ended by then; the effects of the Depression must have just been beginning to be felt — even in a relatively prosperous town like London. Like most of Canada, London was still an agricultural community and although its economy was not as badly hit as on those on the Prairies (where it was estimated that 30 % of the workforce was then out of work) many families were reduced to poverty. Unemployed men roamed the countryside looking for food, and even middle class families were reduced to living on charity. There was little money left over for recreation; amusements in the Davey household had to be free. The woodlands and farms were nearby; a favourite pastime was to pack a lunch and go hiking or spend all day at the Thames Park swimming pool. In the winter there was skating and tobogganing.

After Grade 8, "Bus" went to Beal technical school to take a motor mechanics course for three years. Here he met Aubrey Johston another boy of his own age and disposition, who was destined to become his best friend. Johnston's family had a farm on the outskirts of London; while there "Bus" developed a great interest in horses, quickly learning to ride.

To the Johnston family, "Bus" was another son; this mutual affection continued into the war years. While he was not overtly religious, like most Canadians of the time, "Bus" and his family attended services every Sunday while their social life centred around the local church. The Anglican Young People's Association organised dances and outings for teenagers and "Bus" became its President. His sisters recall (with some pride) that several of the local girls developed crushes on him, and continued to write to him even when he was posted away with the air force. It was at about this time that he also began to enjoy poetry — not a subject that would have appealed to a teenage boy in motor mechanics class, but a good way of expressing his feelings.

Movies and radio programs were a teenager's main entertainment then. No doubt the Davey family along with the rest of the country listened to the Canadian Broadcasting Corporation's most popular program, *The Happy Gang*. It starred Eddie Allen and Bert Pearl and featured the latest music from below the border interspersed with ad lib humour.

Like most teenagers, "Bus" was car crazy. The one behind him in this photograph was definitely not his Gray Dort!

Photo: Johnston family

There were no jobs for apprentice motor mechanics but "Bus" was luckier than most. On graduation he was taken on at Lawson & Jones, a London printing company. His pay cheque allowed him to buy a car in 1939 — but not much of one. It was a Grey Dort, an old fashioned open tourer that had seen many owners since it rolled out of the factory in 1915. "Bus" overhauled it completely and once it was capable of continuous running, he and a friend, Art Pinches, drove across the border to Detroit. That they made it so far was incredible but while driving around the city the two eighteen-year-olds were twice stopped by the Detroit police. The hard-bitten Detroit cops who probably felt that they had seen everything couldn't get over "that old car" driven all the way from London, Canada.

By 1939, even Canadians were starting to become alarmed at what was happening outside their country. The major powers were rearming, the League of Nations seemed helpless, and war looked inevitable. "Bus" probably got his first inkling about the coming conflict from cinema newsreels . Ever since he could remember, they had been full of comically uniformed dictators exhorting their armies to invade neighbouring countries, and of Spanish towns being destroyed by German bombers. Fascinated by aircraft, "Bus" must also have known that compared to the Fascists, the Royal Canadian Air Force hardly existed. If he saw RCAF fighters at all, they would have been old and slow British castoffs.

Best Friends — Aubrey Johnston and "Bus" Davey in 1940.

Photo: Johnston family

To teenagers like "Bus", Art, and Aubrey, war was part of another world. Few high school students in London, Ontario would have known what the implications of the Anschluss were or who Ethiopian Emperor Haile Selaisse was. Montreal and Toronto apart, Canada was a small-town, homogenous, mainly white society. To the country's eternal shame, the government had stopped all immigration from Europe in the 1930s, and except for the cook at the ubiquitous Chinese restaurant, there were few "foreigners" in London. Not many Londoners had travelled further than Toronto or Windsor and the slaughter in the newsreels must have been difficult to understand. It was still the small town that Stephen Leacock might have modelled his *Sunshine Sketches* on or that the Hollywood director Frank Capra would have used in his movies.

The biggest event to take place in Canada in 1939 was undoubtedly the visit of Their Majesties King George VI and Queen Elizabeth. The city was given its first coat of paint in a decade and people lined up for hours to watch the royal couple flash by. With more than half the country of British descent, the royal visit affirmed their heritage, and possibly the certainty, that Britain and her Empire as the repository of all Western civilisation, were in danger. By 1939, the British government was becoming frantic for allies. The Munich Agreement had failed; the Americans were in an isolationist mood and the remainder of the Empire was too far away to count on. The glamour of royalty apart, the propaganda value of the visit was immeasurable.

As part of their London tour, the King and Queen were driven through the grounds of Westminister Hospital, waving to the patients, most of whom were veterans from the last war. Their motorcade had barely left when an ancient Grey Dort lurched down the same route. It was driven by "Bus" with Art Pinches in the front seat and both their mothers waving regally from the rear as their majesties had done. This moment of pure pleasure was to sustain all the occupants of the car in the sad years ahead. They had a great time and so did the patients.

Canada declared war on the Axis powers on 10 September, 1939. Like the Army and Navy, the Royal Canadian Air Force was woefully undermanned and poorly equipped. Fighters and bombers were expensive to build or buy during the Depression, and there seemed little need for a modern air force with the country protected by oceans on either side and polar regions above. The years of penny-pinching had starved the RCAF of modern aircraft, and what few there were Prime Minister Mackenzie King wanted to keep at home for coastal defence. But the British were in desperate circumstances. Air power whether strategic or defensive demanded vast numbers of air crew and on December 17, 1939, Canada, Britain, Australia and New Zealand signed an agreement in Ottawa that became the British Commonwealth Air Training Plan (BCATP). Simply put, Canada would be used to train the thousands of air crew required to take the war to the enemy.

Across the country, airstrips, hangars and barracks were thrown up to teach the flood of Commonwealth and American volunteers that poured in. Alberta, Manitoba and Saskatchewan were ideal for BCTAP activities — flat land, clear weather and far away from civil or military air activities.

"Bus" enlisted in May, 1940 — he was only eighteen but had a good background in mechanics and wanted to fly in the RCAF. His best friend Aubrey tried to enlist as well, but because he was the only male on the family farm, and as the food produced was vital to the war effort, he was turned down. Like all the recruits, "Bus" must have wanted to fly Spitfires immediately in the Battle of Britain. But before he could be sent to a flying training school, he had to report to an RCAF Manning Depot. Here the recruits got their first taste of the service and learned the air force regulations, discipline and drill. As boring as this might have been, he also received his first uniform, a plus that helped any young man's chances at getting a date.

He was then posted to No. 1 Technical School St. Thomas, Ontario, for training as an aero mechanic. With the war, London like hundreds of Canadian communities, boomed overnight. It must have seemed that every young man and woman was in some sort of military uniform and those that weren't found their skills in demand in nearby munitions factories. Because of the BCATP, London had become the site for No. 3 Elementary Flying Training School and the locals soon became used to the little yellow Fleet Finch biplanes bobbing over their countryside.

Before 1940, few young people lived away from their parents until they got married. Now not only were they far from home, but had salaries from the military or munitions industries — for most the first money that they had ever seen. This and the sense of being part of a great adventure must have been a heady mix. London was within easy reach of the military bases at Centralia, St. Thomas and Fingal and the city's service clubs and churches were hard pressed to provide entertainment for all the soldiers and airmen on leave. After the dismal Depression, it was a wonderful time to be young. Best of all, the government telegrams that began with the dreaded "We regret to inform you that ..." hadn't begun arriving in any numbers yet.

"Bus" was fortunate to be posted close to London. His family became used to his Friday phone call, announcing that he was coming home on the weekend "with a few friends and could his sisters provide a case of beer and have a few of their girlfriends available?" He loved to sing and dance — the jitterbug had just become popular, and when the airmen got to 13 Southgate the family would roll up the living and dining room rugs and turn on the radio. It was a scene that must have been playing in many households at that time. There would inevitably be a meal and his sister Iris later wondered how Mrs. Davey could feed all of the youngsters.

When the basic training ended, "Bus" was posted to # 8 Air Repair Depot, Winnipeg. The prairie city was renowned for its hospitality to servicemen and "Bus" continued his rounds of the dances and parties. It was here that he also became interested in flying. He attended night school to bring his academic subjects up to the requirements so that he could remuster as a pilot. At No. 10 Service Flying Training School at Dauphin, Manitoba, "Bus" would have learned to fly on a Tiger Moth before graduating to the twin-engined Cessna Crane. Ungainly and bulbous, the Crane was unloved by its pupils because of its homeliness and docility in the air. Learning to fly on the Fairey Battles had some cachet, as after all, they had been used in operations in France and the Harvard was as business-like as most fighters. But the Crane was forgiving and perfect for instrument and night flying.

Through late 1942 "Bus" studied hard to pass his examinations and build up the hours night flying. He was night flying every second night from 12:00 to 4:00 and also attended Ground School at noon, so sleep was minimal. There was little time to enjoy the fleshpots in Winnipeg now.

When "Bus" returned home on leave he told his sister Iris that one of his most memorable experiences was flying solo above the clouds and seeing the shadow of his aircraft like a cross below him. She asked him if the experience made him feel closer to God and did he ever pray up there. He said "Sometimes I say — Jesus Christ!"

On December 3, 1942, he wrote to Aubrey's mother : "This course is one of the few things in my short life that I have ever been serious about. To get a commission I will have to be near the top in Ground School and get a very high flying mark. We go through the best training in the world for (the wings) Believe me, they don't miss a thing." He wished Aubrey luck in his "night flying" and hoped that he would find "a nice little gal and settle down — but as there were no gals good enough for him, that's out."

He got his Wings in February 1943, and left Dauphin for Summerside, Prince Edward Island, where he received his commission in May. Then he shipped out for Banff, Scotland, the home base for RCAF 404 Maritime Patrol Squadron. The Squadron had formed at Thorney Island in England in 1941 and was tasked with coastal patrol and escorting the torpedo bombers that attacked enemy shipping. Its badge was a Buffalo's head below which was the motto "Ready to Fight". For a young pilot, Coastal Command was not as glamorous as Fighter Command or impressive as Bomber Command but its wartime role of convoy protection was as vital as the other two. The aircraft used were the Stranraer flying boat, the Douglas Digby and Lockheed Hudson, all slow and lumbering, designed as pre-war civil aircraft. But Davey couldn't believe his luck when he was posted to the more lethal side of Coastal Command — the RCAF's anti-shipping marauders.

The 404 Squadron when "Bus" joined, was engaged in escorting convoys along the Norwegian coast and suppressing enemy defence. In December 1942, it had upgraded from its Bristol Blenheims to Beaufighters. The Beaufighter was one of the fastest, most formidable aircraft of World War II, its "bulldog" look giving one the impression of two massive engines with an airplane squeezed between as an after thought. Yet even with the Beaufighter's speed and its 20 mm. cannon, the Squadron sustained heavy losses. Attacking German ships bristling with guns was suicidal and the decision was taken to arm it with rockets. By 1944, enemy sailors hugged the coast and kept a sharp eye out for the

The crew of an RCAF Beaufighter pose for a publicity shot. Given the assignment of attacking enemy ships, the Beaufighters would soon be armed with rockets.

PL-19443

rocket-firing aircraft that swooped down on them almost at sea level. The RCAF's Beaufighters ranged along the European mainland coast, hunting down shipping in Norwegian fjords and French rivers inspite of the barrages of flak from coastal batteries along the shore. Once a squadron aircraft was so low that its crew photographed Norwegian civilians waving at them from the cliffs above!

That summer, 404 was sent to a base in the south of England so that their patrols could concentrate on the French Atlantic coast in preparation for the D-Day landings. It was then that Davey was credited with scoring eight hits on the hull of an armed German merchant ship in Royan harbour at the mouth of the Gironde river. On June 6, 1944, fourteen of the aircraft attacked two German destroyers to prevent them from interfering with the D-Day landings. The raid was a success and the destroyers limped home, badly damaged.

When death came to "Bus", it was from an unexpected quarter. On October 2, 1944, Davey and F/O L. Robinson were forming up over Banff in aircraft #LV 189 for an operational sortie. Also circling was Beaufighter # IZ 444 flown by F/O F.M. Stickel and F/O G.A. Long. The two aircraft collided and Davey's plane crashed three and half miles from the airfield. The accident killed all four of the air crew in both Beaufighters. "Bus" was buried at the cemetery at Banff and the war raged on to its conclusion.

The squadron was disbanded on May 25, 1945. It had sunk four enemy ships, damaged others and shot down fourteen German aircraft. But the cost had been high. It had lost thirty-five of its own aircraft and seventy-seven air crew. In 1951, 404 squadron was reformed at Greenwood, Nova Scotia, as a Maritime Patrol and Training unit and today flies CP-140 Auroras.

On his last visit home before going overseas, "Bus" gave his sister Iris a letter and asked her not to show it to their mother until after he had left. The letter contained a poem entitled *"An Airman's Prayer."* It was in his own handwriting and Mrs. Davey would later keep it in her prayer book. Art Pinches, too, never came home. For their mothers, the day the two boys in the Grey Dort's front seat on the heels of the royal motorcade must have seemed very far away then ...

Iris told a *London Free Press* reporter that they didn't know whether or not "Bus" had written the poem himself but the family kept it to remember him by. It had been published in *Wings Abroad*, the RCAF overseas newspaper and its editor wrote "that a thorough check had disclosed no previous authorship."

Iris has always felt that "Bus" had a premonition that he wasn't coming back home to London. When flying operationally he couldn't write about what he was actually doing and the censor made sure that he didn't tell them about the anti-shipping sorties in his Beaufighter. He did write that he had looked up his parent's families in the old country and discovered hundreds of cousins in England but thousands in Wales. In one final letter he said that when he came home, they would all have a big party. He added if he didn't make it, they should have the party anyway because he would be there with them.

"Bus"'s war was every bit as ferocious as his father's at Ypres, and that he chose to "join up" might be incomprehensible to us today. After all, the tyranny of Fascism was far away from his hometown and he wasn't conscripted. As we all do, the fun-loving young Londoner feared death, but he consciously chose to fight evil — in complete disregard for his own life. A lesser man, knowing the odds, would have been content with flying safer missions. More than eleven thousand "Bus" Daveys were lost in the RCAF during World War II, but we are fortunate this young airman's legacy tells us why.

In 1973, Aubrey visited his friend's grave at Banff, Scotland.

Photo: Johnston family

AN AIRMAN'S PRAYER

Almighty and all present power,
Short is the prayer I make to Thee;
I do not ask in battle hour
For any shield to cover me.

The vast unalterable way,
From which the stars do not depart,
May not be turned aside to stay
The bullet flying to my heart.

I seek no help to strike the foe,
I seek no petty victory here;
The enemy I hate, I know
To Thee is dear.

But this I pray, be at my side
When Death is drawing through the sky;
Almighty God, who also died,
Teach me the way that I should die."

Several Londoners contributed to this biography but my special gratitude to: the *London Free Press*, Mr. E.R. Boland for newspaper clippings, Mrs. Marjorie Mennill who boarded with neighbours behind the Davey family home and sent me the photo, Mrs. Iris. Mackie ("Bus"'s oldest sister) for her encouragement, Art Taleski who also attended Beal Tech, Mrs. Mabel Johnston, the widow of "Bus"'s best friend, who also sent me photos and Mrs. Aldene Knight, Aubrey's sister for "Bus"'s letter. This story is yours.

JAMES C. FLOYD
AERONAUTICAL ENGINEER

When apprentice Jim Floyd entered the Manchester factory of A.V. Roe and Co. Ltd.(AVRO) in 1930, he could have had little idea that he was setting out on a journey that would take him to working on the ultimate in supersonic passenger flight — the Concorde. Then, such an aircraft would have seemed to the young man in the realm of science fiction. That he would also emigrate to Canada and be largely responsible for designing the world's first regional jet airliner and leading the team on the controversial Arrow fighter would have been completely inconceivable. But all through his career, Floyd was destined to be in the centre of ambitious aeronautical projects — the Concorde, the Arrow, the C102 Jetliner, CF100 fighter — and in the beginning, the Avro Anson and Lancaster bomber.

James Charles Floyd was born in Manchester, England on 20 October, 1914, growing up close to the Avro factory. He attended the Manchester College of Technology, studying while working four days a week at Avro. The start of the Second World War found him at the Avro design office at Chadderton where a bomber called the Manchester was being built for the Royal Air Force. The RAF needed a long range bomber to carry the war deep into the industrial heart of the Third Reich and the twin-engined Manchester was to be the mainstay of such a force. However, it's Rolls Royce Vulture engines were proving unreliable in flight and difficult to service and Avro's chief designer Roy Chadwick had his team cast around for a better power plant.

The company was also busy building the Anson for coastal patrol and could do without problems of this kind for its next project. Floyd and his two colleagues in Chadwick's high security special projects office were assigned to study alternative engines. One of the options was using four Rolls Royce Merlins. Sir Roy Dobson, the head of Avro, was receptive to

James Floyd in 1949 with a model of the Jetliner.

Photo: James Floyd

the idea and decided to go ahead with the four-engined Merlin version. Not so the British Ministry of Aircraft Production, who wanted Avro to stop work on the Manchester immediately, and retool to build the Halifax bomber instead. When Dobson protested, it was pointed out to him that total production of Merlin engines was allocated to the Spitfires and Hurricanes then being flown in the Battle of Britain. Besides, the four-engined Halifax bomber was about to come into use. But as Floyd recalled with admiration, Dobson, rather like Winston Churchill, was not one to give up. He went to the Rolls Royce company himself and got their promise for a supply of Merlin engines. Then armed with the drawings that Floyd had prepared for Chadwick, he set about convincing the Ministry that with four Merlins the Manchester would not only be better than the Halifax but also be flying by the end of 1940. Having made that assurance, he hurried back to Chadderton and ordered his design and manufacturing teams to get a prototype bomber in the air as soon as possible.

A crash program ensued and a Manchester now with four Merlin engines, made its first flight on January 9, 1941. Its subsequent performance proved Chadwick and his team correct. The Merlins were a perfect compliment to an otherwise excellent aircraft design. The new aircraft was called the Lancaster, and although they were unaware of it, the Chadderton designers had created the legendary British bomber of World War II. More than 7,000 Lancasters would be built, including 430 by the Canadian Victory Aircraft at their Malton factory outside Toronto. In 1944, the young Floyd was made chief projects engineer at the Avro design office in Yorkshire. One of his assignments was to study applications of jet engines to passenger aircraft, a sure sign that peace was near.

When at war's end, the Lancaster factory in Toronto closed down, Dobson decided it would be a perfect location to build a range of aircraft for the North American market. From bombed out Britain, Canada seemed a land of great promise, where there were opportunities for an indigenous aircraft industry close to the American market. Displaying the doggedness that enabled him to get the Merlins, Dobson had A.V.Roe Canada Ltd. in business by December 1, 1945. He also managed to convince some of the best engineers at the British plant to join the Toronto company. Jim Floyd was one of them, casting his lot with Avro Canada to become first its chief design engineer and later vice president of engineering.

Dobson shrewdly knew that the Americans with their experience and industrial capability had captured the market in piston-engined airliners. The Douglas DC-4 and the Lockheed Constellation both conceived before the Second World War, were far ahead of anything that the British or Canadians could begin to design in 1945. Instead, Avro took a quantum leap into the unknown world of airliners that would be powered by jet engines. It was a bold step. As Geoffrey de Havilland in England was to find out with his Comet, the concept of jet travel was so radical that no one really knew very much about it. At a time when the RAF and RCAF were still learning to fly the rudimentary Vampires, Avro wanted to take fifty civilians, seat them in comfort in a pressurised cocoon and then catapult them to twice the height that passenger aircraft then cruised at! It was such a bold move and so fraught with risk that even the giant Boeing and Douglas companies would not attempt it until almost a decade later.

The Avro project to design and build a jet airliner was encouraged by a requirement put out by Trans-Canada Airlines. The government-owned airline was then making-do with Avro Lancastrians (a civil version of the bomber) on its trans-Atlantic run that were poor competition for the American Constellations. The C102 jet transport as the Avro prototype was called, emerged from the drawing boards far ahead of its contemporaries. Almost five decades later, it would not be out of place among the Boeing 767s and DC-9s of today. The aircraft was designed to take up to fifty passengers, cruise at 450 mph with a top speed of 500 mph. Floyd and his team first wanted to power the aircraft with Rolls Royce AJ65 engines, but when these were unavailable, they substituted four Rolls Royce Derwent 5 jet engines instead, pairing them in pods under each wing so that when more modern engines became available, they could be incorporated without major change in the aircraft's structure.

As innovative as the Avro team was, it must be remembered that in the 1940s all calculations to design aircraft were done using simple slide rules and logarithm tables. Computers were still far in the future, and Floyd credits the youthful enthusiasm of his design team and their manufacturing colleagues, with completing the prototype in so short a time. Finally on a hot August 10th, 1949, the propellerless transport was presented to the media outside the Avro plant at Malton for its first flight. Emblazoned across it's fuselage was the snappy title Jetliner — the first time such a word was used. The maiden flight went without mishap and the two test pilots, Jimmy Orrell and Don Rogers, were enthusiastic about the Jetliner's smooth handling.

Everyone in the crowd at Malton to watch the flight, must have been aware that Britain's de Havilland had flown the world's first passenger jet two weeks before. But this was a first for Canada — and the young company. For once the Americans had been left far behind. No one was to know that it would be a full five years before Boeing's 707 would take to the air. For his part in the successful of designing and developing of the first North American jet transport, James C. Floyd was awarded the

Wright Brothers Medal in 1950 — the first non-American to receive it. That year he would also become a naturalised Canadian.

Despite its initial enthusiasm, Trans-Canada Airlines had grown leery of the idea of a pure jet transport and now chose to opt out of the project completely. The Derwent engines had a higher fuel consumption than the Rolls Royce AJ65s which would affect the aircraft's payload and range. To TCA, having reserve fuel was critical and this was the reason the airline gave for opting out of its order for Jetliners.

Jet operation with all it entailed was too radical a concept for a government airline that had been founded by bureaucrats. Gordon McGregor, the president of TCA would later say that the reason his airline turned down the Jetliner was that it was trying to struggle out of debt and could not afford so expensive an aircraft. If Avro was going to blame them for the debacle, TCA pointed out that there had never been a formal contract to actually buy Jetliners. Besides it was busily engaged in equipping itself with the new Canadair NorthStars. Subsequently, it became common knowledge that the federal Transport Minister C.D. Howe, the acknowledged czar of aviation in Canada had a vehement dislike for Avro's creation. Howe had firmly tied TCA to Canadair of Montreal for NorthStars. The tiny national aviation industry and airline could not support two indigenous airliners simultaneously and the

The Jetliner at the Hughes airfield at Culver City, California.

Howard Hughes

Howard Hughes stands by the Jetliner for an exclusive picture taken by Don Rogers.

Don Rogers

Jetliner was effectively orphaned. In 1951, Ottawa ordered that all work on the C102 cease and that Avro concentrate on building fighter aircraft for the Korean War.

To recoup its investment, the company realised that the market for the Jetliner was going to have to be below the border. Avro arranged for a promotional tour for the Jetliner to be staged between Toronto and cities in the United States. Canadian and American media reported that the Canadian jet transport flew from Toronto to New York in under an hour — half the time that piston-engined aircraft took. It wasn't long before American airlines began to take notice. National Airlines of Miami signed a letter of intent to purchase four Jetliners with an optional six more later. The aviation pioneer Howard Hughes, owner of Trans World Airlines, had the Jetliner flown to his airport at Culver City, California, for closer examination and even took the controls of it himself. Whatever his later eccentricities, Hughes always had an eye for promising aircraft designs and immediately saw the potential in the Jetliner. He commended Floyd on his aircraft and was keen to buy thirty of them for TWA. This caused both United and Eastern airlines, close rivals of TWA, to show an interest as well. Perhaps the highest complement of all came from the United States Air Force, an organisation that rarely buys non-American aircraft. It's procurement department took the unprecedented step of allocating funds for the possible purchase of twenty Jetliners for high-altitude navigational training.

Floyd's team was also responsible for the Avro CF-100, Canuck. Called "the Clunk" or "Lead Sled", the last CF-100 was retired from RCAF service in 1981.

DND/REC 75-928

Floyd and his team at Malton were now working on a second prototype — a version that could carry sixty passengers and use American-built jet engines. But it was all for naught. The Canadian government had lost patience with Avro and ordered the C102 program cancelled. The factory was to be retooled for mass production of the CF-100 Canuck, the RCAF's Cold War fighter. Sadly, the prototype became the only Jetliner to ever built. It haunted the airport for years to be used as a chase plane until in 1956 it too was scrapped. Only the nose remains for future generations to admire at the National Aviation Museum in Ottawa. The Jetliner has come to symbolize national timidity and remind us that for a brief moment Canada held the lead in jet travel.

At the same time Floyd was occupied with another Avro masterpiece — the Arrow. More has been written about this aircraft than any other in Canadian aeronautical history. In October 1958, Floyd himself would explain in a lecture to the prestigious British Royal Aeronautical Society that the Arrow had been born out of national insecurity. During the Second World War, Canada had suffered from a loneliness complex. It had always been dependent on either the British or Americans for front-line aircraft. Even Canadian-built Hurricanes, rather than being used for home-defence when the Japanese were attacking the Aleutians, were allocated by London and Washington to the Soviet Union.

To prevent this from ever re-occurring, in 1946, the Canadian government had taken the uncharacteristically bold step of deciding to design and build an indigenous fighter aircraft. The RCAF needed to re-equip its defence squadrons, then flying outdated Mustangs, with a twin-engined, all-weather jet fighter. Contemporary military strategy held that the next war would take place high over the polar regions with invading Soviet bombers on their way to lay waste to North American cities. Tracked by a chain of radar installations, Canadian fighters would scramble to intercept them. Reluctant to rely on American-built aircraft, the Canadian government asked Avro to design and produce an indigenous aircraft. The company's directors must have seen this as the first step to designing a dynasty of Canadian fighter aircraft that would do for Avro what the Avenger did for Grumman. The result was the CF-100 Canuck; Avro built 700 of them for the RCAF and the Belgian Air Force. It took six years, from the start of the design in 1946 to delivery of the first aircraft to the RCAF squadrons. The mainstay of Canada's contribution to the North Atlantic Air Defence ((NORAD), the Canuck has become part of our national aviation folklore, even its faults are recalled by those who flew it with a mixture of humour and pride.

Floyd had become chief engineer in early 1952 and was now deeply into the rescue of the CF-100 fighter program. In addition to his responsibility for setting up the design team activities to reduce weight and correct structural deficiencies that were showing up in the RCAF testing programs, he was now responsible for the operations of the experimental manufacturing teams, with a mandate to take the first batch of CF-100 aircraft back, modify them and return them to the RCAF in double quick time.

Avro would not be as successful in its next project, which would take on a life of its own, figuring prominently in the annals of Canadian aviation history. In 1952, as the Cold War deepened, the RCAF realised that the CF-100 was quickly becoming obsolescent and that it would have to be replaced by a supersonic fighter very soon. To meet the Russian bombers high over the Arctic called for an aircraft considerably more advanced than the Canuck. In May of the following year, the government issued a directive for a design of such a fighter. The

On August 10, 1949, Floyd's Jetliner, the first passenger jet in North America, took to the air from Malton.

PL-50431

specification called for a two seat, twin-engined aircraft with phenomenal performance that would not only have to include a large armament bay, but also carry enough fuel for the range required.

Chief engineer Jim Floyd knew from the outset that in order to satisfy the RCAF need, an entirely new aircraft would have to be designed. Like his old boss Chadwick, Floyd assembled a team of engineers that matched his own brilliance and drive. They drew up a plan for a tailless delta with very thin wings that could carry the large fuel capacity needed. The project was designated the CF-105.

Avro felt that the conventional methods of building prototype aircraft with minimum tooling and then pre-production models with more sophisticated tools would not work with the CF-105. A radical change in philosophy was necessary. Because of the timetable that the RCAF had set Avro, the decision was taken to build entire production aircraft from the outset to save time. All layout drawings were made full scale to become masters for tooling templates. He would later write that "permanent type tools were made up throughout the build of assembly jigs, sub-assembly jigs and detail tools." It was expected that there would be problems finding suitable engines for the aircraft. Several were planned but rejected for one reason or another and the Avro team had to re-design the fuselage many times to accommodate the characteristics of each.

Finally, it was decided to fit the first five CF-105s with Pratt and Whitney J.75s and from the sixth on with higher powered and lighter Orenda Iroquois engines. The first run-up of engines took pace on 4 December, 1957, and the taxi trials started on Christmas Eve. The CF-105 was christened the Arrow and in the four years since it had first taken shape, achieved more publicity than any aircraft ever built in Canada, either before or since. Weighing as much as a World War II Flying Fortress, it could exceed Mach 2 and climb to 60,000 feet in four minutes. The term "hype" was still thirty years away, but to the employees at Avro, it must have seemed that the media reported every detail of the aircraft's gestation. While the members of Parliament debated over the need for such an expensive fighter to protect Canadian airspace when a cheaper guided missile might do as well, the cost overruns caused by the specification changes attracted heavy criticism, especially from the Opposition. There were more than 650 subcontractors and millions of dollars involved and every change or delay received maximum public attention.

Whatever the political controversies, the Avro Arrow was a technical success, vindicating for Floyd the abandonment of his Jetliner five years before.

PCN-217

At 9:51 AM on 25 March, 1958, Avro's test pilot Jan Zurakowski, took the Arrow into the air, flying for thirty-five minutes over Toronto. On his third flight, he broke through the sound barrier. Zurakowski and the other test pilots that flew the Arrow said that the aircraft's handling characteristics "agreed well with the estimates." In September, when Zurakowski flew the third Arrow, he broke the sound barrier on the first flight.

To Jim Floyd, the Arrow's first flight must have vindicated the abandonment of the Jetliner five years before. Modestly, Floyd always draws attention to the team of engineers that he directed, rather than his own role in the Arrow's development. But the Canadian Aeronautical Institute knew otherwise. In 1958, Floyd was presented with the J.A.D. McCurdy Award for the part he played in bringing Canada's most ambitious aeronautical projects to fruition. That year, the British Royal Aeronautical Society asked him to deliver the Commonwealth Lecture on the design of the Arrow. That October also saw the first British and American jet airliners begin scheduled services, a technological feat that must have made Floyd wonder at "what-might-have-been" for Canada. Still, the Avro Arrow was a technical success. The RCAF wanted 150 of the aircraft and the newspapers proclaimed that once the fighter was equipped with the advanced weapons system Astra 1, neither the Russians nor Americans could match it.

But once more fate in the guise of Ottawa stepped in. On 20 February, 1959, Prime Minister John Diefenbaker opted for a guided missile defence rather than manned interceptors and cancelled the complete Arrow and Iroquois projects. The prime minister announced in the House of Commons at 9:30 AM that day that the development of the Avro Arrow and the Orenda Iroquois engine was to be terminated immediately. To prevent the Arrow from ever being revived, the federal government also ordered that all six aircraft, all tools, jigs and drawings be destroyed.

"Black Friday" had a devastating effect on Avro. Fifteen minutes before the decision was made public, the Department of Defence had called the factory with the news. By 10:15 AM it had spread around the company, from Jan Zurakowski and the test pilots, to the secretaries to the shop floor. This was the second time that a project in which the young company had invested so much time, money, talent and pride had been killed off by the government. This time the wound was fatal and all 14,000 Avro employees were laid off.

Floyd was as devastated as any of his colleagues, but spent the weeks that followed touring the potential aviation employers in the United States looking to find work for his staff. Mainly through his efforts (and the fact that their achievements were well-known) many of the Arrow team were snapped up by Boeing, Lockheed, North American, Douglas and other companies. The breakup of Avro coincided with the Race for the Moon and the Americans jumped at the opportunity to recruit the talented Canadians for their space program. Some twenty-six of Floyd's team were recruited by NASA to work on what would ultimately become the Mercury, Gemini and Apollo programs.

For Floyd there was no dearth of job offers, and because he had remained in contact with British scientists also interested in supersonic flight, he and five of the Avro team were soon working for Hawker Siddeley Aviation in England. His new job description could have been written by himself. He was appointed chief engineer of an Advanced Projects Group to do a feasibility study for a proposed British supersonic transport (SST). While concentrating on this, the Hawker-Siddeley think tank would also study all other possible forms of flight, from vertical and short take-off and landing (VTOL and STOL) to nuclear-powered aircraft. In 1959, the British Government awarded a contract for a joint feasibility study to Hawker-Siddeley and Bristol Aircraft for an SST. Unrestricted in their pursuits, the Floyd think-tank also worked on orbital vehicles and an innovative SST that would not make a sonic boom. For his work on supersonic technology, the Royal Aeronautical Society awarded Jim Floyd the George Taylor Gold medal in 1961. He maintains that had he been allowed to pursue the no sonic boom supersonic aircraft project, the resulting aircraft like the Jetliner, would have changed airline travel from that time on. But by now the British had opted to build the Concorde in partnership with the French and there was little interest in another version of an SST.

In 1962, Floyd left Hawker Siddeley to establish his consulting firm, J.C. Floyd and Associates with offices in Epsom and Esher, Surrey. Knowing of his experience in supersonics and transportation, the British Ministry of Aviation hired him as a consultant for the Concorde. By the time the Concorde went into service in 1976, Floyd's company had carried out over sixty major studies on the operational use of the SST. It would not be until 1978 that the veteran designer would actually fly in the Concorde from London to New York and back. Incorporating many of the features that he had worked on — in Canada or England, Floyd's thoughts must surely have turned to some of his other achievements, the Jetliner and Arrow. When he retired in 1980, Floyd and his family returned to Toronto where he now devotes most of his time to passing on the story of Canada's aviation heritage to another generation of Canadians — although he did take time out to write a book about his favourite aircraft — the C102 Jetliner.

One of Jim Floyd's proudest moments was in 1988 when the University of North Dakota hosted a special conference of aerospace scientists, sponsored by NASA and other international aerospace agencies from around the world to discuss the future of hypersonic flight in the 21st century. Floyd was invited to present a landmark paper in advanced aircraft design that he had written twenty-seven years before in 1961. At the conclusion of the conference, a special banquet was held to honour Jim Floyd. One of the attendees at the conference, the honourary president of the Scientific Teachers Association of Ontario remembered: "My most vivid memory of that event was how revered Jim Floyd was in that company of experts. He was in fact the living symbol of the proud legacy this nation (Canada) has carved in aviation history." After the banquet Floyd was presented with a lifetime of achievement award by the Air Industries Association of Canada (AIAC). In 1993, Canada's Aviation Hall of Fame inducted Floyd for among other things, "his superb organisational skills in the field of aeronautical engineering that have been of lasting benefit to Canadian aviation."

In his 1985 memoirs, Frederick T. Smye, the former president of Avro and Floyd's immediate boss, remembered "Jim Floyd, as chief engineer, assumed the ultimate technical responsibility throughout the continuing development of the CF-100. As vice-president of engineering he also assumed the awesome responsibility for the Arrow. In complete dedication, he led the teams which provided Canada with world leadership in aeronautical technology, only to be discarded by successive governments."

The honours and awards for a lifetime of advancing passenger travel continue to come to Jim Floyd throughout his retirement, but perhaps the most notable took place on February 3, 1984, when the United States Space Shuttle Challenger carried into space a special plaque with a citation in the name of J.C. Floyd. Oh Canada!

Phil Garratt influenced the birth of the legendary Canadian bush planes, the DHC-2 Beaver and DHC-3 Otter.

De Havilland/Canadair Archives

PHILIP CLARKE GARRATT
OF DE HAVILLAND CANADA

P.C. (Phil) Garratt exemplified the very best of the Canadian aviation tradition. A pioneer aviator, he was an instructor and a test pilot early in his career. Through three decades as an executive with De Havilland Canada, Garratt profoundly influenced the birth of the legendary bush planes, the DHC-2 Beaver and DHC-3 Otter. Best of all, for all his success, "PCG" was loved by his employees, remaining unassuming and modest all his life.

Like many of his generation, young Philip Clarke Garratt wanted to fly when the First World War broke out. The aircraft's potential was still being debated in 1914, and although the major powers fielded air squadrons as early as 1911, they were seen as reconnaissance units rather than weapons. At the start of the war, J.A.D. McCurdy lobbied hard in Ottawa for the federal government to support an indigenous air arm. He assured Prime Minister Robert Borden that if the Curtiss Aeroplane Co. was given the contract it would train all the pilots and furnish the aircraft for such an air force. But as McCurdy was a friend of Glenn Curtiss and a director in the company, this prejudiced his patriotism and Borden refused the offer. Instead, the Minister for Militia, Colonel Sam Hughes, bought an American-built Burgess-Dunne aircraft and shipped it and three pilots off as part of the Expeditionary Force to Europe. Both Borden and Hughes felt that this was to be the extent of Ottawa's involvement in aviation.

Then in April 1915 the Royal Navy began advertising for trained pilots in Canadian newspapers. The Navy had been charged with protecting the British Isles from attacks by high-flying German zeppelins and needed pilots. As most of the flying schools were in the neutral United States in the Spring of 1915 when Glenn Curtiss and McCurdy opened theirs in Toronto, hundreds of would-be aviators flocked to it. Garratt was selected with nineteen others, and although they could not know, many of his classmates were destined to play pivotal roles in the country's aviation history. W.A. Curtis and Robert Leckie, for example, became Air Vice Marshalls in the Royal Canadian Air Force in the Second World War. The course was run on the Aero Club of America standards as initially all the instructors were American. Garratt and his classmates each paid $400 for the course and upon graduation were reimbursed $365. He first learnt to fly Curtiss F-flying boats at Hanlan's Point in Toronto Harbour, graduating to land planes when he had mastered this.

Long Branch was then a station on the railway line to Niagara and it was there that McCurdy built the Curtiss Flying School's airfield, which became the first airport in Canada. Here, using Curtiss JN-3s made in Buffalo, New York, the novice pilots were taught to land and take off, make figures of eight, and, with the engine turned off, glide safely down to earth. It took an average of 346 minutes of flying time for each pupil to achieve this.

In 1916, Phil Garratt went to France to join 70 Squadron as part of the Royal Flying Corps. However, fortunately for De Havilland Canada, his career as a fighter pilot was short. At a time when novice pilots lasted about six weeks before falling victim to German Fokkers (some of Curtiss Flying School graduates would be shot down by Manfred von Richthofen, the Red Baron himself), Garratt was returned to England where he served out the war as an instructor at the RFC Flying School at Gosport.

When he came back to Canada after the Armistice, like many other pilots, he hoped to be able to earn a living by flying. But commercial aviation was still in its infancy then and there were no airlines or flying schools — there was barely a Canadian air force — for "de-mobbed" pilots to join. Many drifted into barnstorming, and in 1920 Garratt joined Bishop-Barker Aeroplanes. The two great Canadian air aces, Billy Bishop and William George Barker, both awarded the Victoria Cross, tried to make flying commercially viable and began their own air company to transport wealthy sportsmen from Toronto to the Muskokas. Although Bishop and Barker were very enthusiastic, it wasn't long before the enterprise went bankrupt. In 1922, Garratt left to become an instructor at Camp Borden in the newly-formed Canadian Air Force.

In 1927, the Department of National Defence announced that it was going to help establish flying clubs across Canada. Any community or group that could supply an airfield, a hangar, an instructor and thirty members who wanted to learn to fly, would receive from Ottawa a grant of one hundred dollars for each graduate — and two light aircraft. The scheme was an instant success and by 1929, 24 clubs had been formed across the country. Aircraft manufacturers like the British De Havilland Company and the Montreal Curtiss-Reid Co. all sought to sell their planes to the clubs.

Geoffrey De Havilland already had experience with building his D.H. 60 Moths for British flying schools and sent his manager Bob Loader to Toronto set up an assembly plant for them in Canada. Loader arrived in Toronto and heard that the farm belonging to Frank L. Trethewey on the corner of Weston Road and Jane Street was available for purchase. Trethewey was an aviation enthusiast who had hosted the 1910 Aerial Meet when Count De Lesseps demonstrated the first flying machine Toronto had seen. Since then, the farm had been known as "De Lesseps Field." When De Havilland bought it there was a railway line and a disused canning factory on the property, and both were used in the shipping and assembling of the aircraft. On March 6, 1928 construction began on a hangar where the first two Cirrus Moths from England were put together. The new hangar was painted with the words "Moth Aeroplanes" with "The De Havilland Aircraft of Canada" below.

By then, Phil Garratt was an owner of a chemical company, but in 1928 he persuaded De Havilland to take him on as a part-time test and ferry pilot. The Depression hurt the aviation industry, and in spite of the publicity when the Australian Bert Hinkler used a D.H. Puss Moth to cross the Atlantic Ocean in 1931, sales fell off rapidly. In England, Geoffrey De Havilland developed what historians consider his masterpiece — the D.H. 82 Tiger Moth — and plans were made to assemble it in Toronto.

By 1935, Garratt had risen to the rank of company director and he wound up his chemical business to devote his life to flying. He was a popular manager who knew every employee by his first name and did not believe in rank or specific job descriptions. A job was done in whatever time was needed to do it, which included lunch hours and weekends. During the lean prewar years the company survived because it was run as a family affair. Its director could be counted on to help out on

like Federal Aircraft and Canada Car & Foundry closed their aviation divisions forever while others like Noorduyn were absorbed into Canadair. Garratt returned to Downsview and kept the company personnel together by doing overhauls on Cansos and running off fifty-three prewar-design D.H. Fox Moths. As they could carry three passengers in enclosed comfort, they could be sold to operators of small airlines.

The war's end left many unemployed veteran pilots with their "de-mobbed" savings and dreams of owning an airline. Anticipating this, Fairchild Industries had built the "Husky". Although most pilots bought war-surplus aircraft from Crown Assets Disposal, Max Ward, the future airline operator, wanted new aircraft to begin his own "Polaris Air Charter" with. In 1946, Ward saved up $6,000 and caught the Trans-Canada Airlines flight from Edmonton to Toronto, showing up at Downsview one day to buy a Fox Moth. To appeal to the bush pilot market, Garratt had Canadianised the Moth with the more powerful 145 hp engine, strengthening the cabin floor for freight and enlarging the left-hand door.

But there were still too many old Ansons and Bellancas around for De Havilland's Moth to sell in profitable numbers, so Garratt built a basic flight trainer to replace the Tiger Moths and Harvards that the world's air forces were then using. Named after the chattering rodents outside his Muskoka cottage, the perky DHC-1 Chipmunk made its first flight in 1946 and was sold immediately to the RCAF. In a happy turnabout, the parent De Havilland in England built 1,000 of the Canadian aircraft for the Royal Air Force and the Portuguese made sixty under licence.

The decade of the 1950s saw the building of massive natural resource and defence projects like Kitimat in British Columbia and the construction of the DEW Line across northern Canada. Aircraft came to play an increasingly important part in both projects and small bush outfits sprung up. By now the Norsemen and Fairchilds were obsolescent and the Fox Moths were too small and underpowered. The war had brought to the company a team of brilliant aero engineers like Fred Buller and Dick Hiscocks. They were joined by the veteran bush pilot "Punch" Dickins who left Canadian Pacific Airlines to develop the ultimate bush plane.

De Havilland's chief engineer was the Polish immigrant Wsiewood

"Jaki" Jakimiuk who had designed the high wing Polish fighters in the late 1930s. The DHC-2 Beaver had many fathers, but the credit for its birth must go to Garratt and Jakimiuk. The high-wing, all metal utility aircraft made its maiden flight on August 16, 1947 and was marketed in North America by the Second World War air ace Russ Bannock, the man Churchill called the "Angel of London".

It has been said that the Beaver flew best where flying was the worst. The Beaver suited the Ontario Provincial Air Service as it could be used on floats, skis and wheels and could be flown as a water bomber as well. The United States Army used Beavers in Korea and Vietnam, while the British Army used theirs in Laos, Borneo, and the Middle East. The Australians used theirs on Antarctic expeditions. Beavers were bought by the air forces of Argentina, Cambodia, Chile, Colombia, Cuba, Holland, Ghana, Finland, Kenya, New Zealand and Zambia. In 1956, Phil Garratt was given the 1,000th Beaver off the production line so that he could commute daily from his home in Muskoka. He had CF-PCG

The DHC-2 Beaver was the original "Flying Jeep". It was flown by fourteen air forces around the world, including the Royal Australian Air Force which used this one in Antarctica.

De Havilland/Canadair Archives

painted on the plane in canary yellow. By the time production ceased in 1967, 1, 692 Beavers had been built at Downsview.

With the Beaver, De Havilland knew that it had found its niche market. Not far away at Malton, Avro was building the controversial Arrow, doomed to cancellation because of the expense. Garratt chose not to enter the risky field of jet aviation and concentrated instead on turning out descendants of the sturdy Beaver. The author Sean Rossiter, who wrote *The Immortal Beaver: The World's Greatest Bush Plane* says that there are more Beavers flying today than there were ten years ago. This is because the potential market for bush planes remains very small and the development costs for a new plane are large. The other reason is that the original Beavers, like the DC-3s, will not die off. Hundreds are being reconditioned by specialty firms today, at a cost of $400,000 per plane — ten times their original price ensuring that the workhorse of bush flying will continue well into the next century.

In 1965, De Havilland began making Turbo-Beavers, upgrading the radial engine with a turboprop one, which could operate on aviation kerosene instead of avgas. It also strengthened the wings, bracing struts and tail unit and increased the seating capacity to eight. But because there were so many of the radial engined Beavers about, production stopped after the 60th Turbo-Beaver was built.

The Ontario Provincial Air Service once more indicated that if De Havilland would build a larger, more powerful bush plane, it would buy twenty. This led to the DHC-3 Otter's first flight on December 12, 1951. With a Pratt & Whitney 600 hp Wasp engine, it could seat eleven and lift off with almost two tons of freight. Pilots appreciated its Short-Take-Off-and-Landing (STOL) capabilities, which enabled them to get in and out of the smallest airstrips. Like the Beaver, the Otter acquired a reputation for being able to take off overloaded, fly in weather conditions that would close airports down, and still bring the pilot safely home. Once more, the DHC aircraft was ordered by the U.S. Army, as well as by the military in Canada, Australia, India, Ghana and Norway. Otters were operated by the Australian airline QANTAS deep in the New Guinea jungle and had the honour of becoming Canadian Pacific Airlines' last bush planes. When production ended in 1967, 466 Otters had been built.

In 1962, the parent company De Havilland, never having recovered from the failure of its Comet airplane, was bought by Hawker Siddeley, whose chairman was the former head of Avro, Sir Roy Dobson. He

When the Ontario Provincial Air Service wanted a larger, more powerful bush plane, De Havilland Canada produced the DHC-3 Otter. Bought by the U.S. Army for use in Alaska, it was the last bush plane that Canadian Pacific Airlines would fly.

De Havilland/Canadair Archives

ordered the Canadian branch to take over the old Avro plant at Malton where the Avro Arrow had been built. Garratt, who never liked losing the intimate atmosphere of a small company was reluctant to do so. Dobson convinced Garratt to make wings for the Douglas DC-9 at Malton, a project that he did not like. De Havilland Canada was now deeply involved with designing the twin-engined aircraft that were going to shape its future: the DHC-4 Caribou freighter, the DHC-5 Buffalo and the DHC-6 Twin Otter. Garratt had been at the helm of the company for almost three decades now and was awarded the Trans-Canada (McKee) Trophy twice, in 1951 and again in 1965. In 1960 he also received the Canadian Aeronautics and Space Institute's McCurdy Award. He had the satisfaction of knowing that with the U.S. military involvement in Vietnam, the DHC-5 Buffalo was earning high praise and sales were exceeding all expectations.

These were years of labour strife at Downsview but worse was to come. Before they were taken over by Hawker Siddeley, the British companies De Havilland and Avro had entered the small airliner market with the 125 and the Avro 748. Both aircraft were potential competitors

Philip Clarke Garratt **69**

Garratt lived to see the DHC-5 Buffalo freighter used extensively. Here, its amazing STOL properties are demonstrated at a downtown Manhattan Park.

to the DHC Twin Otter and the chance of being closed down must have been very real to the Canadian employees.

Phil Garratt retired in 1965 but remained on the De Havilland board until 1971 when he was awarded the Canada Medal. When he finally left, De Havilland Canada was on the auction block. Hawker Siddeley was looking to unload its troublesome Canadian branch as soon as it could find a buyer. The federal government, in the process of buying Canadair in Montreal, embarked on a rationalization program of the Canadian aviation industry and on May 27, 1974, De Havilland Canada was bought from its British owners for $38 million.

Paul Garratt died at the age of eighty on November 16, 1974, even as the prototype of the four-engined DHC-7 Dash 7 was being built. He had guided his company from the assembly of Tiger Moths to the world's first quiet STOL airliner. Throughout he had remained unassuming of his role and whatever the circumstances, remained on good terms with his employees. The Beaver, Otter and Buffalo made Canada a world-leader in STOL aviation, their timelessness attesting to Garratt's foresight and aeronautical genius.

C.D. HOWE
MISTER TRANS-CANADA AIRLINES

For his creation of Trans-Canada Airlines, C.D. Howe was the first Canadian to be awarded the prestigious Guggenheim Aviation Medal. Previous recipients included the great aviators like Orville Wright. Although he was not a pilot and had no knowledge of aerodynamics, Howe's pragmatism and hard-nosed philosophy affected airline growth in this country for four decades.

Clarence Decatur Howe was born in Waltham, Massachusetts on 15 January, 1886, the son of a house builder. Not well-off themselves, the Howes were members of a prominent New England clan that had some Canadian connections. Clarence's ancestors numbered Julia Ward Howe who wrote *The Battle Hymn of the Republic*, Elias Howe who invented the sewing machine, and in Canada, Joseph Howe, one of Nova Scotia's leading politicians. Clarence's high school motto was Deeds not Words. It would go a long way in explaining him in later years when he encountered the red tape in Ottawa's infamous bureaucracy. Howe was not a brilliant student but managed to attain a passing grade to get into engineering at Boston Tech as the Massachusetts Institute of Technology was then more commonly called. When he graduated in 1908, at the age of twenty-two, he accepted a teaching position at Dalhousie University in Halifax, Nova Scotia. His annual salary of $2,000 was more than his father had ever made building houses, but more importantly for Howe, the teaching position carried with it an academic prestige that his mother, a former teacher herself, must have rejoiced in.

His entry onto the Canadian political scene began by chance in 1912. Robert Borden, the local member of Parliament was elected prime minister and through his influence, Howe found himself in Fort William, Ontario, building grain elevator terminals for the government. Canada at the turn of the century had become the breadbasket of the

British Empire and industrialised Europe and wheat grown on the prairies was consolidated in elevators at Fort William, Ontario to await shipment overseas. So delighted was the young man with the new job and his adopted country, that he immediately applied to become a British citizen, as all Canadians then were.

But when it came to looking for a bride, Clarence Howe returned to his hometown of Waltham, Mass. He proposed to one of his sister's friends, Alice Worcester, and they were married in 1916, honeymooning at Lake Louise in the Rockies.

H.J. Symington, president of TCA, left and C.D. Howe, right with the first North Star behind them in 1946.

Air Canada Archives

Once the elevators had been built, Howe started his own elevator construction company to take advantage of the bumper wheat crops of the late 1920s. His reputation for decisiveness and innate political cunning made the C.D. Howe Company moderately prosperous. When the Depression caused the wheat market to collapse, Howe like hundreds of others, lost his company but was still well-off. In 1934, he entered another profession — politics. He won the Port Arthur seat for the Liberals in the 1935 election and was invited by Prime Minister Mackenzie King to become the Minister of Marine and Railways.

Howe and aviation had come of age together. When he was a young teacher in Nova Scotia, J.A.D. McCurdy had flown the *Silver Dart*, the first aircraft in Canada. After the First World War, commercial aviation in Canada was seriously neglected by the only institutions that could have nurtured it: the federal government and the railways. Ottawa made it very clear to returning Royal Flying Corps veterans who started their own companies that commercial air operations had to be self-sustaining. As a result by 1930, there were too many small operators vying for too little business.

The government subsidised a few flying clubs, handed out some airmail contracts, and began carving a number of airfields out of the bush in 1929 as part of the Trans-Canada Airway, but this was the extent of its participation.

Ottawa's penny-pinching was in direct contrast to governments in Europe and the United States who viewed airlines and aircraft manufacturing companies as instruments of national prestige and social engineering. Aviation was financially subsidised for flying the flag as Imperial Airways and Air France did, or keeping aircraft builders solvent for their military potential as in National Socialist Germany. The most air minded nation was the United States, where in 1934, government encouragement made possible the advent of the first modern airliner, the Boeing 247, which could fly from coast-to-coast in nineteen hours.

While in opposition, the Mackenzie King Liberals warned that if nothing was done soon to encourage commercial aviation in Canada, American private enterprise would seize the opportunity to fill the void. Prime Minister R.B. Bennett had encouraged air companies in Quebec and Ontario with airmail contracts and, by 1931, it was possible to fly between Moncton, New Brunswick and Edmonton, Alberta. But with the Depression settling in, the airmail contracts were cancelled or given over to the RCAF and the airlines were pushed to bankruptcy.

When he was re-elected, Mackenzie King created a Department of Transport, consolidating the nation's marine, railway and air services into one portfolio, and appointed C.D. Howe as its minister. Howe plunged in and immediately had to contend with a vocal lobby of entrepreneurs who had invested in those struggling air companies as they had the Liberal coffers, and now expected that the new government would reward them with lucrative business contracts. The most prominent of these was the Winnipeg businessman, James Richardson. As the owner of Canadian Airways, the largest air company in Canada, Richardson had been led to believe by Bennett that if ever a national airline was sanctioned, his would be it. But when the Canadian Airway's airmail contracts were cut, Richardson switched his support to Mackenzie King's party. With its victory, he was confident that Canadian Airways would be made the national air carrier. It had the routes, the pilots and the aircraft, and both the Canadian Pacific and Canadian National railways had shares in it.

The new minister was directly opposed to Richardson's expectations. One of most the expensive burdens of the Railway Age in Canada, Howe said, was the financing of two transcontinental lines in a country that could barely afford one. His opinion of the private and public sectors owed much to his New England religious upbringing. Private enterprise to him was associated with greed, the public sector with inefficient bureaucratic bungling. Both had to be controlled by the government. During the 1930s, authoritarian socialism in various degrees was accepted both in North America and Europe. Strong-minded men like Roosevelt, Hitler or Stalin vested all national enterprise in their own hands. Howe was of the same mold, albeit a more genial one. The over built railway system and undercapitalised aviation companies had kept Canadian transportation far behind that of the United States and Europe and always an engineer, Howe's yardstick to anything was: how efficient was it?

He decided that there should only be a single airline to connect the major cities of Canada from coast-to-coast and that it would be government-owned. In June 1936, Howe left for the United States to study their advanced aviation industry. During the parliamentary summer recess, he adventurously flew from New York to Los Angeles in a bone-jarring, ear-splitting Ford Tri-Motor. He met both Juan Trippe, the legendary head of Pan American Airways, and Eddie Rickenbacker, the First World War air ace who later became president of Eastern Airlines, and discussed starting an airline with both of them.

With his mind made up, Howe returned to Ottawa and proposed a bill to Parliament to create a national airline by Dominion Day 1937. It would be called Trans-Canada Airlines and would strive always to be profitable. Both railways would have equal shares in it with whatever private aviation interests that each might nominate. There would be nine directors on the governing board, three from each railway and three from the government. If there were losses, Ottawa would only guarantee them only for a period of two years. Trans-Canada Airlines (TCA) was to be the government's flagship carrier, its chosen instrument in the air, and would compete against all foreign and domestic air carriers.

The president of the Canadian Pacific Railway, Sir Edward Beatty, wrote to Howe, objecting strongly to the composition of the board stating that with only three votes, his company would always be in a minority position against Howe and the CNR. To no one's surprise, he refused to participate in the birth of Trans-Canada Airlines, leaving it's future to the federal government and the Canadian National Railway. Richardson also refused a seat on the TCA board and an offer to co-operate with feeder lines from his own routes. He did however, sell TCA three of his aircraft, and give up Canadian Airway's Vancouver to Seattle service which became the government airline's first route. Howe even succeeded in luring some of Richardson's experienced staff away from him. There was never any doubt that this was to be Howe's airline. When one member of Parliament attacked him about it, saying that this public enterprise smacked of socialism, Howe countered with "It's not public enterprise, it's my enterprise!"

On April 10, 1937, the passing of the Trans-Canada Air Lines Act gave Canada its national airline. True, it was a ward of the Crown and a poor relation to the giant Canadian National, which would do its marketing and ticketing, but in the misery of the Depression, TCA was a tangible symbol of the country's aeronautical ambitions.

The bill had passed through Parliament with some criticism. The new airline's president might be Samuel Hungerford, the president of CNR, but Howe had given several of the most senior positions in the airline to Americans. His response to this criticism was that nationality

The dawn-to-dusk flight at St. Hubert airport, July 30, 1937. Howe is sixth from the left, with the pilot, J.H. Tudhope, on his right, and J.A. Wilson, the controller of civil aviation, is third from the right.

was immaterial, that William Van Horne who had built the Canadian railways had not been Canadian and that the CPR's own previous president, Thomas Shaughnessy was American. Besides, he felt that there were no Canadians qualified to run a trans-continental airline[1].

But by the early summer of 1937, the deadline for TCA's start looked far from being met — the pilots and ground crew were still being trained in California on the Lockheeds that the Minister had personally ordered. One of the problems the Canadians had was adapting to the Lockheed 10s, then the fastest transports in the world. Used to wood and canvas fixed-wheel biplanes that had no flaps or retractable undercarriages, the TCA pilots' training was taking longer than expected.

To deflect any adverse publicity from his pet project, Howe came up with a flamboyant stunt. He ordered his staff to accompany him on a well-publicised dawn-to-dusk flight from Montreal to Vancouver on 30

---

1   Plus ça change ... on May 14, 1995, when the outgoing CEO and president of Air Canada, Hollis Harris, named a fellow Georgian, Lamar Durrett, as his successor, angry shareholders questioned why the airline couldn't find a Canadian to run it.

The publicity flight came close to disaster. Although the Lockheed 12A had a reserve fuel tank fitted, because of the fog, two refueling stops were missed, and the plane landed at Sioux Lookout, Ontario, dangerously low on fuel.

Air Canada Archives

July. The saga of the flight has become part of Canada's aviation history. The aircraft to be used was the Department of Transport's new Lockheed 12A CF-CCT [2] and the pilot chosen for the flight was the celebrated aviation pioneer, Squadron Leader J.H. "Tuddy" Tudhope of the RCAF.

The very early morning of July 30 was dark, rainy and forbidding at St. Hubert Airport. With the Ottawa delegation aboard, Tudhope took off at 4:01AM EDT into the deteriorating weather over Montreal. An experienced pilot and navigator, Tudhope decided it was too dangerous to fly, landed and promptly put the aircraft away in the hangar. In the midst of a thunderstorm, Howe told him to have it wheeled out once more. Then he ordered what must have been the thoroughly unwilling passengers into it. They left again at 5:18 AM, made it to their first refuelling stop, an emergency airfield at Gillies near North Bay, Ontario. After that the cloud cover was so thick that they missed the second one at Kapuskasing and flew on to try and find a gap in the clouds to land at Sioux Lookout.

By now the frightened (and very green) passengers were probably wondering if they would ever see their offices again. Tudhope spent a lot of the flight on his knees poring over the map trying to figure out where they were. When he thought that they might be over Sioux Lookout, he took a chance and steered the aircraft through the clouds. As luck (or his

---

2   Now at the National Avaiation Museum, Ottawa.

calculations) would have it, the town lay directly beneath them, to the relief of all on board. There were three more stops — Winnipeg, Manitoba, Regina, Saskatchewan, Lethbridge, Alberta, and finally, Vancouver.

Thunderstorms followed the party across the country and even the Lockheed's reserve fuel tank almost ran dry. But for the others, the worst must have been watching the minister making a show of casually reading his papers and smoking his pipe through it all. That he could work through the papers in his briefcase while all around him were airsick, is part of the Howe legend.

The little airliner skimmed over the Rockies in high turbulence and it took all of Tudhope's skill to keep it level. To climb any higher meant encountering the pilot's worst enemy — icing. The early bush pilots had already calculated that to avoid ice building up on their aircraft's wing, they had to fly at a minimum of 11,000 feet. However, to clear the Rockies, an altitude of 12,000 feet must be maintained. This balancing act between icing and slamming into a peak in poor visibility, made for a tense flight for all aboard.

After a total flying time of fourteen hours and thirty minutes, CF-CCT landed at Sea Island Airport, Vancouver, on July 29, seventeen hours after leaving St. Hubert. Howe disembarked, beaming to the news cameras like the politician he was. When James Richardson who had considerable experience with cross-country flying, read of the publicity stunt, he said that it was a miracle that they were not reading the obituaries of all aboard in the papers and that why this man Howe wished to advertise his ignorance on so many subjects was difficult to understand.

On September 1, 1937, Howe's airline opened for business. Flown by Billy Wells and Maurice McGregor, a metallic-silver Lockheed 10 A, with Trans-Canada Airlines painted over the passenger door, took off from Sea Island Airport, Vancouver for Seattle. TCA charged the passengers $7.90 for flying them the 122 miles between the two cities The Seattle newspapers covered the event with the banner headline: "Elaborate ceremonies greet Canadian plane." Unfortunately, the newspaper disgraced itself by concluding that this was an extension of the "British airway system." More importantly for Canadian history, on March 6, 1938, TCA started flying regularly between Vancouver and Winnipeg, and on December 1, continued this to Montreal. It had truly become a transcontinental airline.

Once TCA was launched, Howe let his hand-picked managers run it, but kept the airline as part of his personal empire. Even when he made his friend Herb Symington its president in 1941, he somehow justified retaining control of TCA as part of his ministerial wartime portfolio.

At the start of the Second World War, Prime Minister Mackenzie King was astute enough to appoint Howe Minister of Munitions and Supply. At fifty-four years of age, "C.D." was at the height of his powers — his growl as feared in the House of Commons as was his abruptness was in its corridors. He gathered around him what were called the "dollar a year men." They were in their late thirties, too old for the military, who had made their mark in business and now like Howe, could implement reforms and methods into the national economy that would have been unthinkable in peacetime. He overworked, cowed and abused them but after the war, all were proud to say that their mentor had been C.D. Howe himself.

The French surrendered in June 1940, leaving Britain and her distant colonies alone in their fight against the Nazis. Howe knew that the British would be looking to Canada to supply them with munitions, ships, trucks, but especially aircraft and pilots. Whatever modern fighters that Canada's tiny air force flew were already shipped across the ocean. But with German submarines threatening the Atlantic supply lines, the British need for aircraft and pilots was growing more desperate by the day.

There was no time to put contracts out to tender or manufacture armaments on a peacetime schedule. To bypass the pre-war bureaucracy and ram the orders through, Howe made himself the virtual czar of all industry in Canada. He personally controlled twenty-eight crown corporations; he phoned presidents of steel companies in Quebec, timber barons in British Columbia and shipping magnates in Halifax, trying first persuasion and then bullying to get what he wanted.

He had heard that Ralph Bell the president of a Halifax fishing company was an amateur pilot, and phoned him on a fishing vacation. Would he like to be the Director-General of Aircraft Production? Shocked, Bell stammered and said that while he flew his own small aircraft, he knew nothing about actually making them. Howe snapped that wasn't his question, would he take charge of the manufacturing all aircraft in Canada? Bell couldn't refuse.

Ever the showman, Howe was personally present at the openings of most of the new aircraft factories and airfields in Canada. If he couldn't make it, he was either represented by a cheque to pay for it, or as in the opening of Ottawa Airport, by his wife. He loved to say that Canadian industry needed one big project all the time to keep it going ... and he made sure of that. The Avro Anson training aircraft chosen by the British Commonwealth Air Training Plan could not be brought over in sufficient quantities from England, so Howe established Federal Aircraft Limited in Montreal to oversee its production in Canada. Then he passed out contracts ("like playing cards" his critics said), to build parts of the plane to various Canadian companies: Canadian Car & Foundry, de Havilland, National Steel Car Corp., Macdonald Brothers Aircraft and Massey-Harris. Today his methods would be attacked as patronage, his style as bullying, but in the desperate years of 1941-2, he created an aviation industry almost overnight.

He became increasingly frustrated with the British who kept changing their minds as to what sort of aircraft they wanted Canada to build — as the factories were tooling up to build trainers, they were told to retool for fighters and later for long-range bombers. He had a well-founded suspicion that they were trying to safeguard their own aircraft industry when the war was won. On 6 December 1940, to deal with London's munitions bureaucrats personally, Howe took a ship to England.

This was at the height of the U-boat battles and eight days later, his ship *Western Prince* was torpedoed three hundred miles off Iceland. A foreign correspondent for the *Manchester Guardian* newspaper would later report that as the lifeboats were pulling away from the sinking ship, the U-boat surfaced. In spite of the fear and excitement of the moment, the reporter glimpsed an old man with craggy black eyebrows shaking his fist at the submarine's conning tower. It was his introduction to the unsinkable C.D. Howe.

Those in the lifeboats knew their chances of surviving even a few days in the icy Atlantic were slim. All were civilians, well past their youth who had no stamina to cope with the cold of the high seas. In Ottawa, Howe had already been written off. The minister's office began taking phone calls from reporters who wanted details of his obituary. Even Prime Minister Mackenzie King who should have known better, started to think of a replacement for his Minister of Munitions.

On the afternoon of the next day, the shipwrecked survivors saw a tramp steamer come into view. Its Scottish captain had seen the *Western*

Prince go down, and although it meant returning to the U-boat infested waters, he left the convoy to save them. For disobeying orders, he would later be severely disciplined by the Admiralty.

Howe disembarked from the tramp steamer at Liverpool to be met by an anxious Canadian High Commissioner, Vincent Massey. He was invited to spend the night at Chequers, Winston Churchill's residence, and still later was received at Buckingham Palace by the King. Everyone wanted to hear of his rescue. Realising his importance to Canadian industry, the British sent him home in the battleship *King George V,* and when his train finally pulled into Ottawa's station, the whole Cabinet was on the platform to meet him. The house builder's son from Waltham, Mass. was visibly moved at this show of respect.

Through the hectic early years of the war, Howe, like Lord Beaverbrook in London, guided the munitions-producing machinery through mountains of red tape and bureaucratic bungling. He never let either interfere in accomplishing a project — be it securing a single aircraft engine — as he would for a small bush airline, or the massive undertaking of the British Commonwealth Air Training Plan (BCATP). He tirelessly prodded, swore and ran over all obstacles. Historians later would single him out as one of the men who made the BCATP happen in record time. His favourite line was that "He was working harder than a whore running two beds." By 1941, he had his finger in so many pies that the press dubbed him the "Minister of Everything."

From his lair at "Number One, Temporary Building" overlooking the Ottawa River, the minister hurled thunderbolts at bureaucrats and businessmen, stopping at nothing in his efforts to rebuild the Canadian economy. Canada could do anything, he used to say, the war was proving that. He also boasted that his employees were like a team of huskies — an occasional crack of the whip did them a lot of good.

Problems, Howe maintained, were solutions in disguise and the wartime trans-Atlantic air service was exactly that. In 1935, Canada had agreed with Britain and the United States not to launch its own air service across the Atlantic ocean and thus compete with the Imperial Airways' and Pan Americans' flying boats. As it had no aircraft or airline of its own then, this was not a difficult agreement for Ottawa to sign. But by 1941, with thousands of Canadian troops overseas, military mail was piling up by the ton at the flying boat base at Shediac, New Brunswick. With their own priorities, neither British nor American aircraft passing through had room for Canadian mail anymore. Vincent Massey wrote to Howe, pointing out that because of the lack of mail the morale of Canadian troops stationed in England was very low and asked if he could do something about it.

Howe could authorize his TCA Lockheeds to take the mail as far as Gander, Newfoundland but only a long-range airliner could carry it all the way across to England. He cast around for such an aircraft. The most suitable were the American-built Liberator bombers, but the Royal Air Force and United States Army Air Force had priority over them. TCA engineers in Montreal were already servicing the BOAC Liberators used to carry the ferry pilots (several of whom were TCA crew) back to Canada, so the airline did have experience with such aircraft.

The problem was solved in typical Howe fashion; he cast around for anything that would fly the ocean. Victory Aircraft Ltd. in Toronto were about to manufacture Lancaster bombers but it would be months before one was available for Trans-Canada Airlines to use across the Atlantic. To help with the manufacture of the Lancasters, the British had sent a pattern aircraft to Victory Aircraft to be used by their engineers. Once they had finished with it, Howe exercised his authority to have it kept in Canada. Fuel tanks were installed in the bomb bay and the front turret removed for cargo space. Designated TCA-100, and confusingly called a Lancastrian, it began flying from Dorval to Prestwick, Scotland, on 22 July 1943, with eight official passengers and 3,600 pounds of forces' mail. The company was called the Canadian Government Trans-Atlantic Service (CTGAS), and although the passengers did not pay any fares to TCA, this was the beginning of the airline's Atlantic service. On October 8, 1943, Howe himself accompanied by Symington took the flight to Britain — the crossing taking eleven hours and fifty-six minutes. The Royal Canadian Air Force would have liked TCA's Atlantic service put under their jurisdiction, but Howe jealously guarded his airline from the military.

By the war's end there were seven Lancastrians, manned by Trans-Canada Airlines' crews flying three round trips weekly between Montreal and Prestwick. By July, 1945, tickets were being sold to civilians and while no one doubted that the comfort aboard was minimal, CGTAS was the start of Trans-Canada Airlines as a true international airline. Given that the British would become postwar competitors on the Atlantic route, it seems ironic that it was one of their own aircraft that got TCA started.

A TCA Lancastrian at Dorval airport in 1945. This plane was a bomber
built at Victory Aircraft at Malton; it was modified for passengers with its
front gun turret removed to make a cargo hold.

When in 1943, the Allies began to discuss aviation in the postwar
world, Howe attended the Commonwealth Air Conference in London,
and as a result of deliberation there and later the following year in
Chicago, was instrumental in helping set up the international air
organisations of ICAO and IATA. He drafted the basic rules for the
Canadian delegation, ensuring that TCA's Herb Symington was elected
the first president of IATA.

In 1944, with the war definitely drawing to a close, the minister set
about selling off aircraft and airports through his War Assets
Corporation. Thanks to his efforts, the Canadian aviation industry was
then in high gear, turning out Lancaster bombers, training aircraft and
Canso flying boats. Because of Howe the country's defence production
was fourth among the Allies, behind the United States, the Soviet Union
and Britain. Howe now let it be known that the government would
continue to support only those plants that could be converted to
producing civil aircraft — thus killing off some old firms like Canada
Car & Foundry and Fairchild.

His Trans-Canada Airlines had ended the war with the unexpected asset of Atlantic flying experience — more than most of the American airlines had. But to entice fare-paying passengers in peacetime, it desperately needed a commercially attractive aircraft. Making do with converted bombers in 1945 hardly made Howe's airline serious competition to the graceful, soundproofed, upholstered Constellations that British Overseas Airways Corporation and Pan American flew. He concentrated on a plan for a Canadian-made civil airliner for the postwar market. Government-owned Canadian Vickers in Montreal was scheduled to begin work on the Lincoln bomber, but with the war drawing to a close, Ben Franklin, its general manager, lobbied Howe for the opportunity. Franklin was a friend of American aviation icons like Eddie Rickenbaker and Donald Douglas and possibly Howe (although he was no relation to his famous namesake) recognised his own Yankee drive in him. Howe telephoned the head of A.V. Roe (formerly Victory Aircraft) at Malton and persuaded him to take over production of the Lincoln and allow Vickers (soon to become Canadair) to build the first Canadian airliner.

In a move that amazed many, Howe then shrewdly sold Vickers to the American Electric Boat Company which invested $2 million in retooling it. It was a good deal, he said to his critics because it gave Canada access to the latest American technology.

The indigenous airliner was the North Star, a hybrid of four British engines powering an American airframe. The minister personally made the arrangements with Douglas Aircraft in Los Angeles to licence-build their DC-4 fuselage, and Rolls Royce in England for their Merlin engines. History (and many deafened passengers) have roundly condemned the choice of engine. The liquid-cooled Merlins had been designed by Rolls Royce for Spitfires and Lancasters and were never meant for continuous use in airliners. They were noisy, prone to spark-plug failure, and in constant need of overhaul. Rather than risk them over the Atlantic, even BOAC relied on Pratt & Whitney engines for their aircraft. But Howe, perhaps faithful his lone wartime Lancaster, (and knowing that Merlins could be churned out in Canada), opted for them to power his North Star. On a sunny day in July 20, 1946 with her husband watching, Alice Howe christened the first North Star at the Canadair plant at Cartierville.

The North Star was Canada's first indigenous airliner. Solid and stable, bone-jarring and noisy; it seemed to embody much of C.D. Howe's character.

The first Canadian airliner seemed to embody much of the old minister's character. It was solid and stable, but old-fashioned and noisy. Nevertheless, the North Star was bought by the RCAF, Trans-Canada Air Lines, Canadian Pacific Airlines, and even BOAC who called theirs Argonauts. It put both Canadair and the aviation industry in Canada on a firm footing. Howe himself took the first TCA North Star to London that year to attend the ceremonies marking the betrothal of Princess Elizabeth to Philip Mountbatten.

In 1948, Louis St. Laurent became Prime Minister and appointed C.D. Howe as the Minister of Trade and Commerce. Inevitably the long war years, of fighting corporate presidents and petty bureaucrats had taken their toll on Howe who was older and slower. The Avro Jetliner, the first passenger jet in history, should have appealed to his engineer's mind; it would have a decade before. Observers noted that he seemed less able to cope with a postwar world where Canadian industry and exports were expanding furiously.

But he loved his airline fiercely. When in 1948, Gordon McGregor was made president of TCA, Howe gave him only one instruction: "You keep out of the taxpayer's pocket and I'll stay out of your hair."

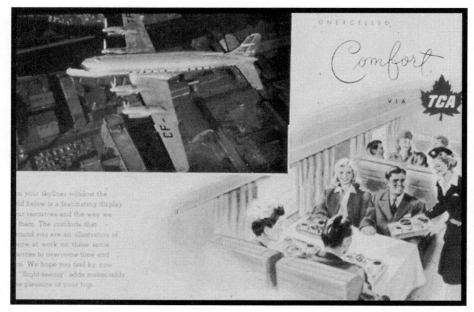

TCA advertisement.

McGregor had good cause to remember this a few months later when he attempted to cut some of the airline's uneconomical routes. The most obvious example of a money-losing flight was between the Ontario Lakehead, and Duluth, Minnesota. A whole aircraft was tied up carrying an average of one and a quarter passengers a day. Lakehead was also C.D. Howe's riding. It must have been with some trepidation that McGregor went to see Howe about this. The minister listened to what he had to say and then raised his eyebrows. Quietly, he asked McGregor if he knew where his riding was. Then instead of an explosion, Howe said "Well, if it's as bad as you say, what are you waiting for ?" It was a move that Howe knew would cost him votes in the next election, but if TCA was suffering, this was a small price to pay.

When Grant McConachie, Canadian Pacific Airlines' president, asked for routes to Australia and New Zealand, Howe guessing that there was no passenger traffic to be had over the Pacific, bestowed his permission in the hope that TCA's only rival would go bankrupt. Canadian Pacific Airlines thrived thanks to the Korean War and McConachie came back to him for permission to fly over the North Pole to Amsterdam — a route that TCA had turned down. Howe once more agreed, peevishly commenting that he hoped CPA's aircraft would be as empty as the regions it was going to fly over.

Rearming the Canadian armed forces to meet the Russian threat, was another matter. The RCAF were making do with World War II Mustangs and a few British Vampire jet fighters, but the Korean War proved that the Communists were better equipped than the West had thought. Should Russian jet bombers ever attack North America, the little Vampires could never climb high enough to intercept, let alone destroy them. In 1951, Howe made it known that he would spend in excess of $5 billion over the next three years, to re-equip the military. This would include designing and building Canada's own fighter aircraft rather than the cheaper option of buying off the shelf. Cost was to be no object. In one of his less fortunate phrases, Howe told the House of Commons "If the army wants a gold-plated piano ... we buy them a gold-plated piano."

The Avro plant in Malton, hurt when the Lincoln bomber contract was cancelled, designed and built the CF-100 fighter aircraft to equip the RCAF squadrons for the Cold War. Because it was outdated by the swiftly moving technology in American aircraft production, the CF-100 became the symbol of Canadian engineering skill, earning nicknames like the "Lead Sled" or "The Clunk". The design and manufacture of a wholly new jet fighter, expensive enough for a superpower, proved to be more costly than the minister realised. But worse was to come.

Encouraged by its CF-100 program, Avro developed a supersonic jet interceptor, the CF-105 — better known as the Arrow. Howe, cautious in his old age, saw production of a Canadian fighter aircraft that had little potential for overseas sales, becoming a bottomless pit. In Parliament, the Opposition shouted that a nascent aviation industry should be building cheap bush aircraft like the De Havilland Beaver instead. When the press reported that the cost of the CF-105 climbed from $1.5 to $2 million per plane to an astronomical $8 million, Howe's phrase of "gold-plated pianos" came back to haunt him. In 1955, he admitted to the House of Commons "I now have to say that we have started on a program of development that gives me the shudders."

Still the astute politician, Howe hurriedly distanced himself from the Arrow and Avro's cost overruns, becoming increasingly concerned with the building of the Trans-Canada gas pipeline. An election was looming in 1957, and he and the Liberals found themselves fighting for their political lives. Never a good speaker, the old man was forced to take to the campaign trail, where his abruptness now earned him boos and catcalls. Born before politicians were supposed to have Kennedy-like charisma, Howe had never tried to cater to the public. His craggy face certainly didn't appeal to viewers on the new medium of television. His enemies compared him and the other old war-horses in the St. Laurent Cabinet to has-beens like Britain and France then embroiled at Suez. On 21 July 1957, after twenty-two years, the impossible had happened. The Liberals were defeated at the polls and Howe was unemployed.

He sold the family home in Rockcliffe and moved to an apartment in downtown Montreal, where he lived out his days by serving on the boards of several companies. Howe's proudest possession was his airline pass — and even after he retired TCA let him keep it.

When in 1959, Prime Minister John Diefenbaker got into political trouble for cancelling the Arrow project and ordering that the six completed fighters be cut up into small pieces, Howe did not join in the condemnation. There were limits, he said to government spending and as he had learned from the CF-100 and the North Star, the aviation industry was an expensive game. Only the superpowers could afford to risk millions on aircraft development.

On 31 December 1960, "C.D." was watching the Saturday night hockey game on television and complained of feeling sick. He retired to bed and that night died of a heart attack.

Howe loved to say he was an American by birth, but a Canadian by choice. Even his fans admitted he was rude and blunt and that he would never survive in a world of political correctness. Creating a Department of Transport and a national airline would have been enough for one lifetime, but these were overshadowed by the wartime crisis of building an industrial complex and the British Commonwealth Air Training Plan. He ran Trans-Canada Airlines as his personal toy and critics remember his answer to customer complaints: "If they don't like it, they can take the train."

Like Winston Churchill, Howe had the misfortune to live beyond his time, and was unable to adapt to a country that he had helped shape. But such was his passion for TCA, that during the war, when he was the absolute ruler of the whole national economy, friends remember him walking down Wellington Street in Ottawa, pointing to a TCA Lockheed far overhead and saying wistfully "Now that is what I would really like to be manager of!"

His child, now called Air Canada, has matured and is now the eighth largest airline in the world. Sixty years after the Vancouver — Seattle hop, it flies to Europe, the United States and the Far East. One summer day in 1957, after he had been defeated at the polls and was contemplating leaving Ottawa, John Baldwin, the Deputy Minister of Transport found Howe sitting on the steps outside the East Block. When he asked if he could do anything, Howe is reputed to have said: "John, promise me, whatever happens, you'll look after Trans-Canada Airlines." Whatever his faults, this country is fortunate that "C.D." chose to live here.

Awarded the Distinguished Flying Cross for his heroic defence of Malta, McNair became the second highest scoring ace in the RCAF.

PL-15946

"BUCK" MᶜNAIR
WORLD WAR II AIR ACE

With sixteen victories in World War II, Robert Wendell McNair cheated death many times, but no event was more amazing than when he fell out of an aircraft in flight. "Buck" McNair had just arrived from Canada in August 1941, to join 411 Squadron at Digby, England as it was in the process of becoming operational. In an open cockpit Magister aircraft, he was sitting behind Pilot Officer W.F. Ash, when he fell asleep, forgetting to put his harness on. Not knowing this, Ash decided to perform some aerobatics and flipped the plane over smartly. McNair woke up to find himself falling upside-down through the air, the aircraft pulling away from him. Fortunately, he had remembered his parachute and pulled its ripcord to land safely.

Robert Wendell "Buck" McNair was born in Springfield, Nova Scotia on 15 May 1919, where his father was employed as a railway engineer. The family moved to Edmonton, Alberta and later Prince Albert, Saskatchewan where Buck was educated. Later he lived at 1546 Victoria Street, North Battleford, Sask. In 1937, McNair was hired by Canadian Airways as a radio operator, to transmit weather information to the company's bush pilots. Two years later, at the start of the Second World War, he tried to join the RCAF as a pilot. But in those heady, early days there was a waiting list to sign up, and it was not until the following year that he was sworn in and posted to the Manning Depot in Toronto. By mid-October 1940, his instructors were so impressed with him that he was selected for pilot training and transferred to No.7 Elementary Flying Training School at Windsor, Ontario. Here he learned to fly the basic Fleet Finch and was moved on to 31 SFTS (Service Flying Training School) at Kingston. On 25 March 1941, McNair graduated as a Pilot Officer.

Luckier than most of his class who were kept in Canada to become instructors in the British Commonwealth Air Training Plan, he was posted to 411 squadron at the Royal Air Force airfield at Digby, in England. The Digby Wing consisted of three squadrons — 266, 411, and 412, all equipped with Spitfire IIs.[1] The Canadians of 411 and 412 affirmed their nationality at the RAF base by erecting a totem pole at the end of the runway.

The pilots' tactics on either side may be partially explained by the aircraft they used. At this stage in the war, the Spitfires IIs that the Canadians flew were only marginally different from the Luftwaffe's Messerschmitts Bf 109s . Both were products of the sport planes of the 1930s, wonderful to fly at medium speeds, but difficult to control in a dive. Enough has been written of the Spitfire's Rolls Royce engine, but at this stage in the war, the Messerschmitt's fuel-injected Daimler-Benz was its equal. The Spitfire pilot had better visibility because of its bubble-hood, while the 109 had an old-fashioned cumbersome canopy that gave the pilot little forward vision. But the 109 had a tighter turning circle than the Spitfire or Hurricane, something that Allied pilots came know in air fighting. On the other hand, the Messerschmitt was structurally weaker than the British fighter and during dogfights, tended to break up in the air if too much stress was put on its airframe. Both aircraft had their deficiencies and even during the Battle of Britain, the British were already developing advanced versions of the Spitfire while the Luftwaffe were testing the deadly Focke Wulf 190.

A month after 411 became operational — during which time an aircraft hit the totem pole and "Buck" had fallen out of the Magister, the Squadron accounted for its first enemy, shot down by McNair. On 10 October 1941, he was flying a convoy protection patrol over the English Channel when the R/T (radio-telephone) crackled with the message that there were 109s from Boulogne below them. This was McNair's first chance to tangle with the Luftwaffe and he dived down to meet them. It was a rash thing for an inexperienced pilot to do, as he discovered. There were seven Luftwaffe fighters circling a downed pilot in the water. He chose one, and started firing on it from 250 yards until he had closed in to about sixty yards. He overshot the disintegrating

---

1 One of the members of 412 squadron was Pilot Officer John Gillespie Magee who wrote *High Flight* the most evocative poem about flying ever written. He was killed in 1941 when his Spitfire collided with another aircraft.

Luftwaffe aircraft and watched his first kill spiraling down. Flushed with victory, he broke away and headed for home ... straight into an ambush. The other Messerschmitts were waiting for him and a burst from one hit the Spitfire's engine. Smoke poured out and McNair weaved about as much as he could, but the Messerschmitt stayed on behind him. When the enemy shot past he was able to return fire, but discovered that only his starboard guns were operating. Somehow his bullets did register and he saw the 109's hood fly off as it began its dive into the sea. By now the Spitfire was in flames and its engine had stopped completely. McNair lost altitude to about 400 feet, levelled and then baled out. Within fifteen minutes, an air/sea rescue launch had picked him up. He had scored his first victory while the second was counted as a "damaged."

When the RAF asked for volunteers for overseas postings — possibly the Middle East, every pilot in 412 wanted to go. The North African campaign was reaching a critical stage as the tanks of the German Afrika Corps pushed closer to Egypt. McNair's luck held and he was one of the two chosen. In February 1942, after sorties over France strafing troops and once a train, he was told to report to 249 Squadron in Malta.

Strategy in the North African theatre had made the British island colony of Malta vital to both the Allies and the Axis. Until the Germans could cope with attacks, all fuel supply convoys for the highly mobile Afrika Korps would continue to be decimated by British air and naval

McNair was posted to 411 Squadron RCAF then equipped with Spitfire IIs. In 1941, he shot down his first enemy aircraft and was himself shot down.

PL-20231

forces from Malta. Like Britain itself, Malta had become an unsinkable aircraft carrier. The island was totally dependent on food and fuel from Britain, and subjected to daily bombing by the Luftwaffe and the Regia Aeronautica from bases in Sicily, only seventy miles away. At this early date in the war, the Mediterranean was a virtual Axis lake, and Malta was effectively sealed off from Allied convoys. The situation became so desperate that it's aerial defence had been whittled down to a few Spitfires, some Hurricanes and the three legendary Gloster Gladiator biplanes dubbed Faith, Hope and Charity. But only the Spitfires could match the Bf 109s and Junkers 88s.

The Luftwaffe began its all out assault against Malta on March, 1942, just as McNair arrived at 249 squadron. He shot down a 109 on 20 March and, six days later, a Junkers 88 bomber as it attacked shipping in Valetta harbour. By the first week of April, the island was fast running out of food and fuel. Its pockmarked airfields could not be repaired quickly enough and the anti-aircraft guns had barely fifteen rounds of ammunition left. The Luftwaffe bombardment was now constant; the whole population of Malta was reduced to living like rats, sleeping in caves and tunnels, existing on scraps of food with even drinking water rationed. Earlier that summer, German airborne troops had taken the island of Crete, and without air cover, the Maltese had no illusions as to what the outcome of this campaign was going to be.

In mid-April, the British could only put six aircraft up to meet the Luftwaffe formations over the battered island. The nearest RAF base at Gibraltar was too far away to fly in more Spitfires, so Whitehall came up with an imaginative plan. The reinforcement fighters would be transported to the Mediterranean by Allied aircraft carriers and launched towards Malta before the Luftwaffe could realise what was taking place. The 700 mile flight over water in a single-engined aircraft was fraught with danger, but the very audaciousness of the project appealed to Prime Minister Winston Churchill. Although the Spitfire was not designed to be stored in a carrier's hold (its wings did not fold) or take off from its deck, it was put into effect. A belly tank for extra fuel was attached to each fighter as were wooden wedges between the flaps and underside of the wings to increase lift for take-off. In great secrecy, the aircraft carriers HMS *Eagle* and USS *Wasp* were packed with the Spitfires and sailed for Malta.

The use of the larger USS *Wasp* was crucial as it had room for more Spitfires below decks. Although the United States was now in the war, the U.S. Navy was reluctant to allow one of its precious aircraft carriers then desperately needed in the Pacific, into the U-boat infested Mediterranean. It took a personal telephone call from Churchill to President Franklin D. Roosevelt for permission to get the use of the *Wasp,* but only for this operation. On 20 April, forty-seven Spitfires were successfully launched from the two carriers. They arrived over Malta, short of fuel, with the Luftwaffe waiting.

Few photos describe the romantic stereotype of a World War 11 fighter pilot better. McNair at 411 Squadron airfield, 5 November, 1941.

PL-4988

McNair and the remnants of 249 Squadron flew constant cover for the incoming aircraft as they landed to be refuelled and armed. In the fierce battles that took place as the Luftwaffe pounced, "Buck" shot down another 109. Despite this, most of the new Spitfires were destroyed while being serviced; Malta seemed doomed to go the way of Crete. Once more Churchill asked Roosevelt for use of the *Wasp* and the two aircraft carriers returned with more Spitfires.[2] On May 9, sixty-two of these were launched and this time the landing and refuelling

2   After its heroic service in the defence of Malta, the USS *Wasp* rushed over to the other side of the world to take part in the Battle of Guadalcanal. On 15 September, 1942, she was torpedoed by a Japanese submarine and sunk.

operation were timed more efficiently. All of them arrived safely, and within thirty-five minutes, were refuelled, armed and airborne to meet a large Italian air force formation making for Valetta harbour. The new aircraft were the first step in the turn of the tide for Malta. Canadians like McNair and H. "Wally" MacLeod of Regina figured prominently in its defence. More famous than either of these two pilots was Montrealer "Buzz" Beurling, who shot down his first Italian Macchi fighter the afternoon he arrived.

During his three month tour on Malta, Flight Lieutenant McNair accounted for seven enemy aircraft and was awarded the Distinguished Flying Cross. Not a natural marksman like Beurling (nor as controversial), McNair's consummate skill was the courage with which he pursued his prey. He demanded the best from his own men, threatening to shoot them down himself if they were careless. When he returned to England and was posted to 411 squadron, his commanding officer noted that the British skies — peaceful when compared with Malta, must have driven him to distraction. More dog fighting was soon to come his way and this time it would be defending Canadians at Dieppe.

The Canadian generals in Britain had been embarrassed by Prime Minister Mackenzie King's refusal to allow them to get involved in North Africa. In the summer of 1942 they agreed to commit their troops to the Dieppe amphibious operations on 19 August. In what would prove a telling argument for fighting under Canadian command, eight RCAF squadrons under RAF command provided air cover for the disastrous landings at Dieppe. The senior Canadian air force officer overseas, Air Vice Marshal Harold Edwards, was not aware of this heavy involvement as Dieppe was a wholly British-run operation. Outnumbered by the Luftwaffe, the RCAF Spitfires shared in the bloody casualties suffered below. McNair's 411 squadron was in constant action over the port and it was the first time that he met the dreaded new fighters, Focke Wulf 190s. He flew four sorties that day, and added two more aircraft to his total.

In September, "Buck" was posted back to Canada as an established ace. He was assigned like Beurling, to touring the country and speaking at war bond rallies. As with Beurling, this must have been painful for a fighter pilot; it would not be until January 1943, that he was sent overseas once more, this time as a Squadron Leader. The squadrons were now organised as fighter wings which would allow them to be moved around wherever they were needed. They flew bomber escorts into

Europe as the German airfields became prime targets. Commanding first 416 and then 421 Squadron (The Red Indians), McNair continued his record of outstanding kills.

His score climbed rapidly during July and August, 1943. Within a month, he had shot down five German fighters. On July 10, he was leading 421 with 403 below when enemy fighters were seen ahead and both squadrons fell upon each other. McNair dived onto one Messerschmitt and, closing on it from astern, destroyed it with one long burst. His opponent's speed, distance and angle of attack was assessed, an instant judgement as to where the enemy was going to be located before McNair fired.

Then his luck ran out. During a sortie over the channel on 28 July, his Spitfire developed engine trouble. Accompanied by his wing man he turned towards home losing altitude from 20,000 feet to 10,000 feet. Then the aircraft burst into flames and McNair put it into a dive to extinguish the fire. In doing so his face was badly burned and he baled out at 5,000 feet. To his horror, as he pulled the ripcord, he discovered that his parachute was also partially burned and he fell almost 3,000 feet before remnants of it blossomed. The heat of the fire had also fused the metal catch on the release handle and "Buck" knew that unless he got rid of the chute, he would be dragged through the waves and drowned. Just before he blacked out, he was able to tear himself loose from the cords. His wing man had already radioed Mayday and continued to orbit around him until other 411 aircraft arrived.

Almost unconscious and without a dinghy, McNair floated in his Mae West for hours until an air-sea rescue Walrus could pick him up. His goggles had saved his eyes; it took him a full three weeks to fly again, his face still heavily bandaged. But his eyesight had become permanently damaged, something that "Buck" tried to keep from his men. McNair's score soon stood at sixteen aircraft shot down and many other probables.

By August, he was back in action, shooting down four more enemy fighters. The others noted that each time he seemed to close in more and more for the kill. What they mistook for stupidity and pride was actually McNair's failing eyesight. It would only be a matter of time before he collided with another aircraft or was himself shot down.

Fortunately, before this could occur, in 1944, he was promoted to Wing Commander of 126 Wing, part of the Second Tactical Air Force and awarded the Distinguished Service Order. The citation read:

"Throughout, Wing Commander McNair has set a magnificent example by his fine fighting spirit, courage and devotion to duty both in the air and on the ground. He has inspired his pilots with confidence and enthusiasm." Now he was too senior to fly in combat, and besides the Luftwaffe was no longer the overwhelming foe it had been at Malta.

After the war, "Buck" remained with the RCAF in England, and was sent to the Empire Flying Training School at Hullavingdon, Wiltshire. On completion of the course in April 1946, he was posted to RAF Fakenham Norfolk to fly the new Meteors and Vampires. He returned to Canada in December having been awarded the French Croix de Guerre with Palm and made a Chevalier of the Legion of Honour.

In the postwar years, "Buck" served as Air Advisor and Attaché of the Military Mission at the Canadian Embassy in Tokyo, a posting that increased in importance as Canadian involvement in the Korean War began. Although he now moved in diplomatic circles, the ex-fighter pilot was no cocktail soldier as his involvement in an air crash in 1953 demonstrated.

Being the Air Attaché at the Embassy in Tokyo, McNair frequently flew through Vancouver Airport, getting a lift in RCAF North Stars carrying troops to the Far East. On 30 December 1953,[3] he was a passenger on a 426 Squadron aircraft returning to Tokyo. Soon after take off from Vancouver Airport, its number four engine overheated and the pilot turned back to the runway. Visibility was bad and heavy icing increased the aircraft's stall speed, causing it to approach the runway too steeply. The nose wheel ploughed into the ground followed by the starboard wing. This broke off and the North Star completely overturned, sliding upside down the whole length of the runway. When it finally groaned to a halt, gasoline was pouring out of the smashed tanks and there was no time to lose in evacuating the aircraft. Although injured and soaked in gasoline, as the senior officer present, "Buck" McNair took charge of this, returning time after time to the North Star's wreckage until all passengers and crew were out. For a year he underwent treatment for spinal injuries suffered and was awarded the Queen's Commendation for Brave Conduct.

In 1956 McNair was promoted to Group Captain and posted to No. 4 Fighter Wing at the RCAF base Baden-Soellingen in Germany. His last

---

3   For a more detailed account of the crash, see author's *Gateways: Airports of Canada* Lawrencetown Beach, Nova Scotia: Pottersfield Press, 1996 pp. 142-3.

operational posting was as Deputy-Commander of NORAD's Duluth sector in 1964. Two years later his battle with cancer began, but instead of retiring "Buck" accepted a posting to the Canadian Joint Staff office at the High Commission in London. He died there on 15 January, 1971 in the country he had helped save. McNair was buried in Brookwood Cemetery among other RCAF pilots killed during the war. Canada's second highest World War II air ace was elected a Member of Canada's Hall of Fame in 1990.

Retiring from Canadian Airlines in 1968, Bob Randall waves from a Fairchild 82B — the type of bush plane he used in 1937.

ROBERT RANDALL
SHRINKING THE POLAR LATITUDES

In the early twentieth century, apart from a few mariners, no one knew what existed north of Alaska and Canada. As late as the 1920s, there was still speculation about a huge land mass in that inhospitable region. Aircraft were the perfect instrument for polar explorers and after the First World War, Roald Amundsen, Richard E. Byrd and Carl Eilson all received credit for their flights over the ice cap. Less well known are the exploits of Robert Randall, a Canadian bush pilot who not only trail-blazed flying in the polar regions but inaugurated Canadian Pacific Airlines' flights from North America over the Pole to Europe.

Robert Cheetham Randall was born in Saskatoon, Saskatchewan on November 2, 1908, a year before Robert Peary first made it to the North Pole on foot. During the First World War an uncle of his served in the Royal Flying Corps and was injured flying a huge Handley Page bomber. Nine-year-old Bob remembers that there was great excitement at the Randall home at 1019 Avenue "A" when they heard of this and it was then that he first thought: "Flying is the life for me!"

Growing up in Saskatoon immediately after the war, he saw aviation pioneer Stan McClelland taking off and landing in his Curtiss JN-4 from a muddy field at 22nd Street and Dundonald Avenue. A former Royal Air Force pilot, McClelland held Commercial Licence No. 2 in Canadian aviation history and flew from Saskatchewan's first airfield which would eventually be named after him. McClelland's aviation business would have died had the Department of National Defense not announced in 1927 a scheme to help establish flying clubs across Canada. Modeled on a British plan, Ottawa's conditions were simple: if a group of local aviation enthusiasts could build an airfield with a hangar and hire an instructor and an air engineer to teach a minimum of thirty people to fly at any one time, the government would give them two aircraft and a grant of $100 for each pupil. It was an ingenious plan that would not only ensure that the country had a nucleus of trained pilots in time of war, but also provide cities with rudimentary airports that they could then develop. Of the sixteen clubs formed across Canada that year the Saskatoon Aero Club was the first to fulfill all the conditions and receive a pair of de Havilland Cirrus Moths.

The summer of 1928 was a wet one when twenty-year-old Bob Randall signed up at the club to get his pilot's licence. When not in the air the young man worked as a ground engineer learning all he could about aero engines. The barren airfield flooded frequently and the ex-Royal Flying Corp instructors muttered that it reminded them of "the mud of Flanders." Former pupils recalled that after a heavy rain the runways would take two days to dry and in desperation the instructors would have the aircraft dragged to one of the neighbouring fields owned by the university and fly from there. With thirty students the demand on the two Moths was high, and the average daily flying time for a pupil was one hour and thirty-seven minutes.

In spite of all the aircraft he has flown in his life, Bob has never forgotten the advice his instructor gave him before his first solo: "if your aircraft is in trouble, remember you haven't got all day and all night to figure out where to land — don't try and turn back to the field — just put her into the trees." On May 25, 1928, *The Star Phoenix* newspaper reported that Bob Randall made his first solo flight in GC-AKG and was going on to do his commercial licence. The Club's instructors celebrated the end of a successful first summer by flying in formation over the Saskatoon Industrial Exhibition, even diving and stunting close to the bleachers. Saskatoon prided itself on being an air-minded city and the club looked for twice as many pupils the next year so that the Government could provide them with two more aircraft.

Once he had built up enough hours and to receive his commercial licence, Bob was hired by Cherry Red Airlines of Prince Albert, Saskatchewan, to fly their Buhl Air Sedan around Lac La Ronge. The Buhl was an American passenger aircraft with an unusual feature for its day: the lower wing was half the size of the upper. The aircraft and the company were not commercial successes and Randall did not stay long with either. It was after all, the Twenties, the heyday of the barnstormer — aerial gypsies who earned a precarious living flying old biplanes from town to town, living off what they could charge for shows and rides.

Randall couldn't resist the lure. That summer he joined two such outfits — Bilby Air Service, and later Duncan Motors. He worked the circuit around Saskatoon, carrying passengers, doing aerobatics and some instructing as well. One of his pupils was a young girl called Hilda Bard who, to Bob's consternation, expressed a desire to do some parachuting from his aircraft. Bob must have been so impressed with this — or possibly to save her from herself, that he married her on August 16, 1930.

Soon a family man, Bob gave up barnstorming and joined Brooks Airways in 1931. He flew Stinsons and Fairchild 71s, doing general bush work that included surveying, freighting fish and forestry patrols. The following year he went to Camp Borden, Ontario, to take the Royal Canadian Air Force course in instrument flying. Most pilots then flew by what they could see — they followed railroads, roads, and even power lines to where they wanted to go. This restricted their operations to daylight hours and good weather. Farsighted people like Bob understood that in order for aircraft to compete with railroads, they had to learn to fly at night, and in poor weather. To his credit, he finished first in the course among other veteran pilots that included Maurice McGregor, Ted Field and Herb Hopson. McGregor would go on to become one of Trans-Canada Airlines original pilots and in 1937, flew their first scheduled flight.

In May 1934, Brooks Airways posted the Randalls to the Yukon. The family fell in love with the North and that fall Bob left Brooks and got a job flying for Northern Airways, based forty miles south of Whitehorse at Carcross on Lake Bennett. With them he flew Fokkers, Super-Universals and the giant Ford Tri-Motor. His flights took him far over the Yukon and northern British Columbia — regions that were then blank spaces on every map, as he pioneered the first mail run between Atlin and Telegraph Creek. The Randalls now had twin boys, Bob Junior, and Ted, who became infected with their parent's enthusiasm for flying.

Bush flying in the 1930s was exactly what it sounds like: you flew over the bush i.e. unmapped territory with little hope of rescue should the plane crash. It required a very resourceful, lucky pilot to make a living out of this work. Not only did the severe climatic conditions of the North work against you, but there were no maps or navigational aids available at this time. There were no railroads or roads to follow and the barren flatness could be disconcerting for a pilot. The difficulties of navigating near the magnetic pole also made compasses unreliable.

Then too, the planes used had their own problems. Because of the limited market, there were no aircraft designed specifically for bush conditions as the Norseman and Beaver would be one day. Even before it took on its payload, a bush aircraft had to have essential emergency equipment stowed on board. This consisted of rations, heavy sleeping bags, a tent, coal oil, shovels, fire pots, snowshoes, engine spares, rifles, and a tarpaulin. It all weighed about seventy-five pounds and detracted considerably from the payload. But in the event of an emergency landing, that extra weight was essential to survival. As there were no radios, the pilot had to be prepared to repair the aircraft himself. Randall's knowledge of aero engines and the spare aircraft parts he carried saved his life and that of his passengers on more than one occasion.

The freight onboard a bush plane was everything imaginable. Prospectors that hired the pilot could only afford a single flight and loaded as much as they could into the aircraft for the long winter. At the frontier towns there were no scales available to weigh the load and the next flight might be six months later. Camping equipment, canoes and food, sleigh dogs and, once even a pair of oxen, were crammed into the cabin. The risks inherent in this practice of overloading the aircraft were very great. Constantly overloaded, the plane's take off runs to become airborne were greater than their manufacturer had designed them to be. This was acceptable with the long rivers and large lakes used but an aircraft straining to get airborne meant an overheated engine or worse failure of that engine at a critical time. Once in the air, the pilot had to make sure that he had enough fuel to get out of bad weather and back to base before nightfall. Although he remains self-depreciating about his career, Randall had joined an elite profession.

In 1935, the American explorer Bradford Washburn, organized a *National Geographic* expedition to survey and map the border between Alaska and Canada. The Saint Elias range of mountains with its glaciers and crevasses discouraged all surface travel by the surveyors of the International Boundary Commission and both Washington and Ottawa encouraged the project. The Alaskan mountains averaged 12,000 feet, with Mount Logan at 19,850 feet, the second highest in North America. The glaciers were immense and one, the Hubbard glacier, extended seventy miles to the sea. With such great distances involved, Washburn chose a ski-equipped plane to carry his expedition and their supplies to base camps in the mountains from where they could work. He was fortunate to get Bob Randall as his pilot.

The expedition arrived at Carcross in early March and had Northern Airways begin flying food and equipment to set up a base camp on the glacier. On March 7, Bob Randall flew Washburn and Robert Bates in the FC-2W2 Fairchild through the heart of the St. Elias range over the great Seward glacier, past Mount Logan to Kluane Lake. The Fairchild was a seven seater of rugged construction with a cabin skylight designed to be an emergency exit in case the aircraft ever sank through ice — an all too frequent occurrence in the spring. It had a service ceiling of 11,000 feet and most pilots would have flown around the mountains, rather than over them. Bob somehow got the aircraft up to 18,000 feet without oxygen, in the bitter cold. To make matters worse, as the aircraft had no camera-well, Bates had the rear door of the cabin removed so that the aerial camera could be used to photograph the terrain. Washburn, Bates and Randall were all aware of the drama of the occasion: that this was the first aircraft to disturb the stillness of the glacier and the majesty of the mountain range. They also understood, that should there be a mechanical failure, there was no hope of rescue.

Randall landed gingerly on the glacier, and Washburn and Bates made camp while he flew off to Kluane to pick up the huskies. He returned with in Washburn's words, "the craziest mass of freight that I had ever seen." Randall sat at the controls and behind him in the small cabin of the plane were sandwiched two men, a dog sled and six huskies! "On our flight that day we made one discovery — that Bob Randall was an amazing pilot" While the teams photographed and surveyed the glacier, Bob kept flying the supplies up from Lake Bennett to the camp. One of his loads, he remembers was 600 pounds of corn meal and beef tallow to keep the dogs fed. By the end of March after the blizzards, Randall flew Washburn and Bates on a photographic flight down the gorges of the Aklsek River to the Pacific. On April 22, Randall and Washburn explored the last unknown wilderness east from Mount Logan, past the unmapped glaciers with rolling hummocks of ice buried beneath the debris of rocks that had fallen on them in avalanches from the mountains. Every major peak was named and photographed; its height and position calculated later, and the boundary between Alaska and Canada fully mapped. In recognition for the valuable assistance he had given which largely contributed to the success of the expedition, Randall was elected a member of the National Geographic Society in April 1935.

Randall left the Yukon in 1937 and joined Mackenzie Air Services (MAS), flying out of Edmonton. Five years before, W. Leigh Brintnell had incorporated the company to provide air services in the Mackenzie district of the Northwest Territories. Brintnell had flown with Western Canada Airways and stayed on when they became Canadian Airways in 1930. He left to form MAS to provide service between Edmonton, Aklavik, Goldfields, (Saskatchewan), Yellowknife, Peace River and Coppermine. The aircraft Bob flew were Bellanca Aircruisers, Norsemen, and Fairchilds.

In 1937, the search for the missing Soviet expedition of Sigismund Levanevsky captured the headlines. On August 12, six Russian explorers led by the veteran explorer Sigismund Levanevsky set out to fly a four-engined aircraft from Moscow across the Pole to Fairbanks, Alaska. It was reported that Levanevsky had taken off from Moscow, made it over the Pole to the Alaskan mainland before disappearing. His last radio message was: "Message No. 19. Motor 34. Flying heavily against 100 kilometre wind, losing altitude from 6,000 meters to 4,300 meters. We are going to land in ..." Then he went off the air.

Randall with the Mackenzie Air Service Bellanca, at Radium Cove, Great Bear Lake, 1938.

Levanevsky became known to the North American public in 1933 when he rescued the American pilot, Jimmy Mattern, when he crashed in Siberia on an around-the-world flight. Newspapers reported that American, Canadian and Russian teams were mounting air/sea rescue operations to locate the Russian aircraft. Specially equipped reconnaissance aircraft and icebreaker ships were said to be on their way from Russia to the Alaskan/Canadian coasts to join in the search. On the basis of the message, the Soviet government directed the search for their aircraft to an area along a line of 148 degrees between the Alaskan coast and the Pole.

For bush pilots, August is the least favourable month to fly in the Arctic — especially with an aircraft fitted with wheels as Levanevsky's had been. The summer rains melted down the ice surface and much of the giant Arctic floes were fragmented, making any landing on wheels impossible. When the Soviet Government asked the British explorer, Sir Hubert Wilkins, to search for their aircraft, he chose to do so in a Catalina flying boat and invited the Canadian air pioneer, Herbert Hollick-Kenyon, to join his crew. Hollick-Kenyon had considerable experience in polar flying, having taken part in the successful search for Col. C.D. McAlpine's expedition in 1928, and the Lincoln Ellsworth Antarctic expedition in 1934.

But even before the Wilkins team began flying north, one lone pilot was already looking for the downed aircraft. On August 14, under contract by the Soviet Embassy in Washington, Leigh Brintnell despatched Bob Randall to the Arctic coast. Chosen for his commercial flying experience in the Yukon and Alaska, Randall used CF-AXM, a Fairchild 82B[1] on pontoons — an improved version of the 71 he had used with Bradford Washburn. With more cargo room and a greater range, the 82B was popular with bush pilots; it was also equipped with a radio. Randall took his mechanic, Gerald Buckham, with him and all the gasoline he could cram into drums in the hold. He began scouting the coastal area around Aklavik, Herschel, Demarcation Point on the Alaskan border and before landing at the Barter Islands in the state itself.

If Levanevsky's heading was anything to go on, it seemed likely that he would have gone down in that area and that some of the natives

---

1 There remains a single Fairchild 82B in Canada. This is CF-AXL at the National Aviation Museum in Ottawa.

would have seen him. Bob landed wherever he saw native groups, asking if they had seen the Soviets. Busy butchering reindeer for their winter food supply, one group said that they thought they had heard an engine; but concluded that it was an outboard motor on a boat. He crisscrossed the area for a full month, making landings to ask about the Russians wherever he saw anyone. He took readings from the sun as his compass was useless. He even made the dangerous 600 hundred mile flight from Aklavik to Point Barrow, Alaska. Only Charles Lindbergh had done this before him on his round-the-world flight.

Randall's meeting with the Russian search team was memorable. He landed the Fairchild on a tiny lake at the Point Barrow settlement and was amazed a few days later when a huge Dornier flying boat with Russian markings touched down. The crew were very friendly, except that they spoke no English, and all the translation had to be done by a Belgian nurse at the settlement, who fortunately knew some Russian. The Dornier was well stocked with vodka which Bob had never tasted before, and amazingly, its hold was filled with cases of French wine. The combination of both, Bob remembers, was lethal. In the spirit of unexpected détente, the Canadian was able to offer a bottle of Scotch to the Russians which they had never tasted before.

The well-publicized search for Levanesky ended without results and the Soviet government retreated into its customary, official silence. Over the years, Randall has often thought that he was looking for someone who was never there. He suspects that in the political climate of the Stalinist regime, the whole scheme was fabricated by the Russians as an excuse to send their aircraft and ships into Alaskan and Canadian territory to spy on settlements in the North. However, for opening up the Arctic coast, the twenty-seven-year-old Bob Randall was made a member of the prestigious Explorer's Club.

In 1940 Randall was promoted to Operations Manager of Mackenzie Air Services and remained in this position when MAS merged with Canadian Airways. The Second World War was the death knell for many bush airlines. Always on the edge of bankruptcy, they now had great difficulties getting new aircraft, adequate fuel, and keeping their trained personnel from joining the armed forces. Brintnell suggested that the country should be carved up into a number of areas with the companies operating in each amalgamated into one organization. However, the intense rivalry between his airline and Canadian Airways run by "Punch"

Dickins, prevented this from happening. This situation allowed Canadian Pacific Air Lines (CPAL)to purchase both companies later that year.

Yukon Southern Transport owned by the flamboyant Grant McConachie was also bought by Canadian Pacific in 1941. To the surprise of many, McConachie was put in charge of the collection of airlines that CPAL now constituted. He had always admired Randall's flying ability, long ago wanting him to captain his old Ford Tri-motor, the flagship of the fleet. Grant never forgot the sight of Bob in an emergency, flying a twin-engined Barkley-Grow on one engine, a feat that until then, thought to be impossible. With more bravado than money, McConachie had fashioned a rudimentary airline out of the bush outfits that he flown with. Like the other air crew, Bob now had a glamorous-looking uniform to wear, radio compasses to home into, and the prospect of job-security. Then the lives of everyone in the Canadian North and Alaska were abruptly changed forever.

On December 7, 1941, the Japanese bombed Pearl Harbour, and the United States and Canada were at war in the Pacific. The American military were aware that the Japanese had a base in the Kuriles near the western tip of the Aleutian islands, and that if the sea lanes to Alaska were threatened, the state would be isolated in its northern wilderness. With the Soviet Union in the war, Alaska and indeed the whole of the north-west, had become strategically important to Washington. An inland air and land route, from Dawson Creek, the Yukon, to Fairbanks, Alaska, safe from Japanese carrier aircraft, suddenly became a priority. In case fuel supplies brought by sea were cut off, a project called the CANOL pipeline to carry oil from Norman Wells to Whitehorse was also begun. Finally, in a feat that would have been physically and politically impossible a year before, hundreds of American aircraft were ferried from Great Falls, Montana, to Fairbanks, and on to the Soviet Union. McConachie's airline because of its considerable experience, was contracted to provide the personnel and aircraft to carry engineers, construction workers and equipment to what became the biggest undertaking since the building of the Panama Canal; the 1,600 mile Alaska Canada Military (ALCAN) highway that linked Alaska and the Yukon to civilization. Bush pilots with Bob Randall's expertise were much in demand and he was loaned to an American company building the Canadian Oil (CANOL) pipeline to organize their flying operations.

After the war, Randall flew from Edmonton as a captain for Canadian

Pacific Air Lines (CPAL) on their domestic routes, using DC-3s. His twin sons got their private pilot's licences with Edmonton Aero Services and in April 1952, became First Officers with CPAL as well. Backed by the resources of the Canadian Pacific Railway, McConachie was able to fulfill his dream of an international network for his airline. He haggled with Ottawa for routes that TCA had no interest in — the Far East, Australia, New Zealand and South America. The Korean War gave him the traffic needed to justify buying Canadair North Stars and later Douglas DC-4s. To access these markets, he moved the airline's headquarters from Montreal to Vancouver. In 1952 Bob Randall was transferred to Vancouver from Edmonton to take over Canadian Pacific's overseas flights which were now using DC-6Bs. This was the airline's first intercontinental pressurized aircraft, able to compete with TCA's Lockheed Constellations. The DC-6Bs were one of the last of the piston-engined workhorses and served the airline until they were replaced by Boeing 737s in 1969. But Bob's favourite aircraft to fly was the DC-6B's replacement on the international routes — the Bristol Britannia, elegantly styled, but an electronic nightmare and the last of the pre-jet airliners.

Scandinavian Airlines System had pioneered an over-the-Pole route with a DC-6B from Copenhagen to Los Angles in 1954 and McConachie was quick to seize on the idea. He knew that a Vancouver-Amsterdam flight would channel people and goods from Europe into the Pacific coast and vice versa. It would be, in his words, "a polar pipeline." When his railway Board of Directors balked at the idea of an airliner flying over the polar icecap, he pointed out to them that as any bush pilot knew, Arctic air held no moisture; it was always clear with unlimited visibility.

On June 3, 1955, CPA's DC-6B CF-CUR took off from Vancouver to Sondestrom, Greenland, and Amsterdam. It's captain was Bob Randall, who must have looked on the white terrain far below with bittersweet memories. Negotiating the St. Elais mountain range with Bradford Washburn, and searching for Levanevsky in his Fairchild, Randall's career had really been the history of aviation exploration in Canada. On June 20, a year later, another polar flight filled Bob with even greater pride when he and his twin sons Bob Jr. and Ted crewed it together to Amsterdam. The *Vancouver Province* newspaper estimated that the chance of this ever happening, due to pilot scheduling, was 1000 to 1.

But the reporter obviously didn't know about the family's aviation heritage. Flying over the polar regions for the Randalls was part of their destiny. Bob's three sons Bob, Ted, and John, and two grandsons, Rob Junior, and Ted Junior, were now all pilot officers in the airline, with his granddaughter an air cadet in the RCAF. In 1986, the Randall dynasty had a combined 135 years of flying time for Canadian Pacific Air Lines totalling 96,600 hours.

Before he retired from Canadian Pacific Air Lines, Bob Randall had flown in excess of 30,000 hours as captain-in-command, in aircraft that ranged from the DC-3s to the DC-8s. He was made a member of Canada's Aviation Hall of Fame in 1973 with the following citation:

" *His pioneer flights over unmapped mountains, and his dedication to purpose during the 1937 aerial search for six Russian fliers, despite adversity, have been of outstanding benefit to Canadian aviation.* "

The flying Randalls of Canadian Airlines. Left to right: son John, a 747 captain; son Bob Sr., a DC-10 captain; Grandson Rob, a 737 captain; Robert Randall; Grandson Ted Jr., a 737 captain; son Ted Sr., a 747 captain.

Canadian Airlines Archives

"Herb" Seagrim was "a pilot's pilot," a founding member of TCA and First Vice President of Air Canada. He is shown here on the left, on June 7, 1966, receiving a gold key from Donald Douglas Jr. in Long Beach, California, prior to taking delivery of CF-TLC, Air Canada's first DC-9.

Air Canada Archives

HERB SEAGRIM
FROM BUSH TO BOARDROOM

"Every man should have one great adventure in his life, one major frontier to overcome," Herb Seagrim once said. "Certainly my great adventure and privilege has been participation in the development of Trans-Canada Airlines."

H.W. "Herb" Seagrim was born in Winnipeg on August 25, 1912 and educated there. As a boy he frequently sat by the Red River watching the RCAF flying boats take off, leaving in their wake the never-to-be-forgotten aroma of doped fabric and castor oil. He started flying in 1931 when an over-eager flying club agent told him that he could learn to fly solo in four hours at a cost of $60. It took Seagrim six hours and he owed the club the difference. Unable to settle the debt in cash, Seagrim made an arrangement with the club to work as a mechanic's helper, and during his off hours he and a friend borrowed a truck and hauled cinders to surface the parking lot until it was paid off.

In 1933, he earned an air engineer's licence and worked for Konnie Johansesson's Flying Service in payment for advanced instruction in aerobatics. With licences in hand in 1935, Seagrim began his career in bush aviation. There were three operators in the province: Canadian Airways Ltd., Starratt Airways, and Wings Ltd. The last was a Winnipeg company that operated a network servicing the mining areas of Flin Flon, Norway House, Ilford and Lac du Bonnet. It used Fairchilds, Fokker Universals and Wacos and advertised that its aircraft were radio-equipped. He received his first assignment almost by default. Wings Ltd. sent him to Regina to rebuild an old Cessna Parasol monoplane which the company had bought after the plane had crashed. After putting the engine and airframe together, Herb flew the finished product to the company's base at Lac du Bonnet. Senior pilots considered it beneath their dignity to fly the peculiar-looking plane, which they had dubbed "The Cesspool".

Herb and his wife hoped to work in "some civilised spot-Kenora or Lac du Bonnet or Hudson, Ontario." However being the most junior in the bush outfit, he was sent to desolate God's Lake, and later Red Lake in northern Manitoba.

As he was the only pilot based at Red Lake, he was constantly flying. There were over sixty active mines in the area and most of them were serviced by air. Seagrim recalls reading that air traffic in the area was so busy that Red Lake had as many take-offs and landings as Chicago Airport.

Passenger traffic was solicited at the beer parlour or at the bootlegger's, as the customers were miners who were either going "out" or returning from visiting the family. The trick was, Seagrim recalls, to get them signed up before they went on a drinking binge and lost all their money.[1]

The local prospector traffic required careful scheduling. "One party would want to be picked up before dark; while another wanted to be picked up at a different lake from the one they had landed at and another might want to stay on a week. If the pilot missed any one of these appointments, he lost business and his reputation."

One day, while flying to Lac du Bonnet in a Fokker Universal, the engine stopped and Seagrim looked for a lake to land in. He came down at Kilborn Lake with his two passengers, his ten-year-old brother and a very sick trapper going outside for an appendix operation. The engine couldn't be fixed, so they lived on the beach for ten days, eating the emergency rations while waiting for rescuers. The trapper, who was supposed to be sick, spent the time chopping wood for the signal fire, while Seagrim worried that he would have to remove his appendix. Finally another Wings Ltd. pilot spotted them, but not before rumours started that burnt wreckage and their bodies had been found, upsetting Seagrim's wife.

On another occasion he arrived from Winnipeg with a passenger on the first flight of the Spring season, flying a Waco with wheels. He had been told by radio that the ice on Red Lake was strong enough to land on but didn't know that the local sawmill operator had run his tugboat across the bay, after which it froze over - but remained thinner than the rest of the lake. As the Waco slowed for the landing run, it plunged through the thin ice and sank up to the upper wing. Seagrim scrambled

1   The primary source of Seagrim's early career is the "WCAM Aviation Review" vol. 20. no. 4. December 1994. pg. 25-30 used by permission of it's editor Shirley Render.

out of the cockpit window on the upper wing and never got wet, but the frozen passenger had to be fished out. Such was the kindness of the frontier community that, without being asked, people came out with planks, timbers and lifting equipment to help. Within hours they had the aircraft out of the water and they spent the next three weeks repairing the machine. The whole town remembered that day as "the day that the airplane went through the ice."

In the mining towns, bootlegging and prostitution were tolerated by the authorities because of the preponderance of unattached males who were lonely, bored or just "thirsty". The Ontario Provincial Police could keep track of both the liquor and the prostitutes as both had to be flown in — and escorted by the police to the saloon or the local madam. She was a kindly person who was known to provide Christmas hampers and even financial help to people down on their luck. "In Red Lake, a nice balance was maintained between praying and sinning." Seagrim remembered. "The big deterrent was being sent outside. Jobs were hard to come by and a trouble-maker lost his means of livelihood."

Then in the fall of 1937, Herb Seagrim applied for a position with Trans-Canada Airlines. He didn't hold out much hope but one day a letter arrived saying that he had been accepted as a pilot, subject to a satisfactory interview. He remembers being nervous at the time about flying those huge twin-engined aircraft but it was a challenge that could not be resisted. At the freeze-up, he and his wife bade farewell to Red Lake and bush flying forever.

On December 6 he began work at TCA and promptly "went under the hood" (learning blindflying) on the Lockheed 10As. What distinguished an airline from a bush outfit was the pilot's ability to fly at night, relying only on instruments, and still keep to a schedule. The year 1938 was made a training one for much of the TCA staff and it would not be until March 1, 1938, that Seagrim would fly the first air mail from Winnipeg to Regina.

During the Second World War, like other TCA captains, he was based in Vancouver as a test pilot for the Boeing overhaul plant. He got his first promotion in 1943 and was made Chief Pilot, Western Region and moved to Lethbridge, where the following year he was made Superintendent of Flight Operations. Most of his job consisted of flight instruction and writing the basic flight procedure manuals, which remained in use with Air Canada well into the jet era.

Early in his airline career, Seagrim's skill as a pilot was severely tested. The Lockheed 14 that he and Captain Bill Barnes were flying from Vancouver over the Rockies to Lethbridge picked up a pilot's worst nightmare — a heavy load of icing. Ice hampers the function not only of the wings but also the propellers, pitot tubes, and carburetters. It disrupts the air flow over them by destroying lift and increasing drag, raising the stalling speed. The only way they could stay in the air without stalling was at full power. Seagrim, worried that the plane's speed could cause them to overshoot the runway, radioed the airport staff at Lethbridge to take down the fences at the end of the runway. They began their descent into Lethbridge knowing that the temperature on the ground was below freezing, but on circling the airport "like a rocket", to their amazement, Herb and Bill saw the ice falling off the wings in chunks. To their joy, they realised that the ice was being melted by a Chinook which had not yet reached ground level.

In 1949, when the TCA headquarters were moved to Montreal, Seagrim was appointed General Manager, Operations. With the postwar boom in aviation, the airline was ready to expand. It had replaced its Lancastrians overseas with North Stars and had outgrown the Lockheeds as a domestic transport. The old planes were too primitive and lacking in endurance: the Lodestar could only carry seventeen passengers, while the Lockeeds had a range of only 800 miles, forcing the airline to maintain refuelling stops across the country. During the war, TCA had stretched them to accommodate four more seats — making them the first "stretched" airliners in history — but with the wartime travel restrictions lifted, they were still too small. Although the larger DC-3s had been available, Seagrim remembered that the Lockheeds had been ordered by the dictatorial C.D. Howe to start the airline, and few would have had the temerity to argue with him!

In 1945, TCA bought the first of 30 DC-3s from the U.S. Aircraft Disposal Board, sending them to Canadair to be refurbished. They were seen as a "stop-gap" airliner until new technology made turboprop aircraft available. Surprisingly, the DC-3s soldiered on in service some three years after the first DC-8 jets were delivered. The last one sold in 1963 with a record 41,000 hours (with TCA alone) on it.

Always known as a "Douglas" man, Herb later wrote of the DC-3, "It would be hard to find a pilot, or a mechanic or in fact a passenger that did not have a soft spot in his heart for the DC-3."

With a seating capacity of thirty passengers, the DC-3 took care of TCA's short/medium routes, remaining in service from 1945 to 1963.

Air Canada Archives

The RCAF war ace Gordon McGregor became president of TCA in 1948, and in his memoirs recalled taking his first flight with Herb Seagrim over a flooded Fraser River. The city of Vancouver was cut off from ground transportation and TCA had garnered favourable publicity by flying food in. C.D. Howe happened to be in Vancouver and accepted McGregor's invitation to fly with him and Captain Seagrim to Winnipeg. Howe wanted to see the extent of the flooding himself, so Seagrim flew the North Star up the Fraser Valley, giving Howe and the other passengers a tour of the flooded regions. McGregor wrote:

> We climbed to a safe altitude to cross the Rockies, approximately 11,000 feet, when Seagrim, who could spot

a game bird at any given distance, drew our attention to a pair of ducks on the exact reciprocal of our course and slightly below us. Most men begin to feel some distress with their breathing at 8,000 feet sitting absolutely still, and that these birds could be rapidly flapping their wings at that height, without benefit of oxygen has remained a matter of wonder to me ever since.

Seagrim got to know Howe quite well when he would fly the minister down to the Bahamas to play golf. The flight crew always enjoyed this as they would be Howe's guests at the old Empress Hotel in Nassau where he played poker.

The Anglophile Gordon McGregor fell in love with the Vickers Viscount at the Farnborough Air Show in 1949. He flew the turboprop aircraft himself, comparing its handling with his wartime Spitfire. This and his friendship with Vickers director George Edwards led to TCA buying a fleet of Viscounts and later its successor, the Vanguard. Seagrim considered the Viscount "too avant-garde" for TCA use and was supported in this by Clayton Glenn, the Aircraft Evaluation engineer. The airline's maintenance department was suffering with the Rolls Royce Merlin engines on the North Stars and complained about the poor British workmanship and the fact that parts cost twice as much as parts from the U.S. suppliers. But regardless of their and Seagrim's opinion, the British aircraft were purchased by TCA and adapted to North American use.

Multi-million dollar aircraft fleet purchases have less to do with technical comparisons than national prestige and keeping aviation industries going — even if these fleets happen to be in foreign countries. The airline took delivery of its Douglas DC-8s in 1961 and began looking around for a short/medium range twin jet to replace its Viscounts. McGregor's friend, Sir George Edwards, knighted for his export orders, now ran British Aircraft Corporation which made the BAC 1-11 jet. Trans-Canada Airlines' staff feared that his influence on McGregor would lead to another unsuitable British airliner being bought. The situation was compounded when French President Charles De Gaulle, hectored Prime Minister Lester Pearson to buy French-made Caravelles, which were older and more expensive than the BAC 1-11s. In the midst of this, Quebec Premier Jean Lesage complained publicly that TCA "should not reject the Caravelle because it was French." The whole issue exploded on national television, when at a parliamentary hearing on the selection of the aircraft, McGregor not knowing that his microphone was on, said "The Caravelle is no good for TCA. Not that I think its any great shakes either." His remarks caused a huge uproar that had students from the University of Montreal picketing TCA offices and the riot police being called out.

Fortunately, calmer heads like Herb Seagrim's (now Senior Vice President-Operations) and Clayton Glenn's prevailed and the British and French options were rejected in favour of the Douglas DC-9. It proved a wise choice as the DC-9s — like their DC-3 parents — were used by airline for the next three decades, long after the BAC 1-11 and Caravelle were forgotten. In 1966, Seagrim was named Executive Vice President of the airline, which had changed its name to Air Canada the year before. Seagrim himself went to the Douglas plant at Long Beach, California himself to accept the first Air Canada DC-9 from Donald Douglas Jr.[1]

Although now in the boardroom, Seagrim still kept his pilot's licence valid, which now included operating the DC-8, explaining that he "always approved of any training that helped executives to better understand their business." In 1969 he was named First Vice President of Air Canada.

Gordon McGregor retired in 1968, and it was expected that Seagrim who had been groomed for the presidency, would take his place. But it was not to be. Prime Minister Trudeau chose Yves Pratte, a lawyer from Quebec City, to be Chairman of the Board of the Crown corporation. Seagrim remained on for a year at the request of Pratte and retired in 1969. He moved to Florida to run a yacht charter business - beginning he says, his third career. He was given a huge farewell party at the Queen Elizabeth Hotel, in Montreal, attended by 300 friends and colleagues. Instead of a gold watch, he received a colour television set, leaving Air Canada on March 31.

Made a Member of the Aviation Hall of Fame and awarded the Order of Canada, Herb Seagrim returned to Montreal two decades later to live in the suburb of Baie d'Urfe. His living room overlooked Lake St. Louis where, while there were no RCAF flying boats taking off, at least this "pilot's pilot" could watch the Air Canada flights coming into Dorval Airport in the distance.

---

1 The selection of Airbuses by the government of Brian Mulroney two decades later proved that the art of airborne intrigue had not died.

Claude Taylor used to say that an airline's face was that of it's employees. From 1976 to 1993, he guided Air Canada through turbulent times.

Air Canada Archives

CLAUDE I. TAYLOR
AIRLINE PRESIDENT

What sea power had meant for the Europeans in the previous century — moving commerce and impressing foreigners — the national airline is to this century. As newly independent Third World governments were quick to grasp, a jumbo jet with the state emblem on its tail, was a powerful symbol of their economic and cultural maturity. By the start of the 1970s, those who had founded the airlines in Canada, icons like James Richardson or Grant McConachie, would hardly have known their handiwork. Their bush outfits that once survived by begging for postal contracts, had evolved into national industries with thousands of employees and had become international showpieces for Canada.

Air Canada like the country itself, was riding the prosperous cycle of years that had begun in 1967. It had bought Boeing 747s in 1971, Lockheed Tristars in 1973, and retired the last of the Viscounts in 1974. An all-jet airline that flew from the Soviet Union to the Caribbean, it also pioneered the use of a Short Take Off and Landing service, connecting Rockliffe Airport in Ottawa with the EXPO 67 parking lot in Montreal. Then events suddenly conspired to change this situation for the whole airline industry. The OPEC oil embargo, labour troubles, terrorism and political interference, crippled airlines the size of British Overseas Airways Corporation and Air Canada was no exception. Running the jewel of the Crown corporations no longer called for a bush or fighter pilot, but an individual with experience in marketing, finance, and most of all, human relations. Fortunately for the airline, Claude I. Taylor became its President in 1976.

Born on May 20, 1925, at Salisbury, New Brunswick, Taylor has always credited his love for aviation with his early neighbours. The farm next door was owned by the parents of Air Vice Marshall Hugh

Campbell of the RCAF. Another boyhood idol was Walt Fowler from nearby Sackville. Fowler had learned to fly in 1928 at Jack Elliott's school in Hamilton, Ontario, and would go on to have an illustrious career at Trans-Canada Airlines[1].

Claude graduated from Salisbury High School in 1941 as the country was in the midst of building airfields for the British Commonwealth Air Training Plan. One of his summer jobs involved bringing water to the construction crew on the building site of an airfield near Moncton. For a high school student, it must have been a heady experience watching the streams of yellow perils or military trainers bob about the airfield.

He attended Robinson Business College and began cycling twenty miles from home to Moncton Airport to watch the TCA Lockheed Lodestars take-off. His mother warned him to prepare himself for the business world and get a job in one of Moncton's three major employers: the T. Eaton Catalogue company, Swift Meat Packers, or the Canadian National Railway workshops. But when he attained the intermediate level in his quest for a Chartered Accountant's certificate, he joined a small retail company in Saint John, New Brunswick, where he met and married it's accountant, Francis Walters, in 1947. The postwar aviation boom was about to begin and Claude knew he had to somehow get into the airlines. The lady he boarded with played bridge with a woman whose son who was the head of TCA in Halifax so it wasn't long before he was called for an interview. Within days, the young man was working for Trans-Canada Airlines in Moncton as a reservations agent on the night shift. A year later, he was posted to the airline's Montreal headquarters as a clerk. He had the ultimate ambition of rising to become the company's chief accountant in Winnipeg.

TCA's president at this time was the legendary Gordon McGregor, a World War II fighter pilot and twice winner of the Webster Trophy for amateur fliers in the 1930s. McGregor presided over the airline through a period of unprecedented growth, as it acquired overseas routes and Lockheed Constellations to compete with British Overseas Airways Corporation on the Atlantic run. Although there were some deficit-plagued years, the former fighter pilot's panache was what the public

---

1 Fowler's career is described in the author's book, *Flying Canucks: Famous Canadian Aviators*, Toronto: Hounslow Press, 1994.

TCA Lodestars at Moncton airport, New Brunswick in 1943, when young Taylor used to cycle twenty miles from home to watch them take off.

Air Canada Archives

admired. He introduced turboprops like the Vickers Viscount to the North American continent, ReserVec computers to the reservations system and in 1960, bought the DC-8, TCA's first jet airliner. Five years after this, Trans-Canada Airlines had such extensive routes outside Canada that its name no longer adequately described it and was changed to Air Canada.

Taylor speaks of McGregor with admiration. He got to know him well since one of his first jobs was to carry the president's briefcase and accompany him to hearings in Ottawa. Men like McGregor, and Juan Trippe of Pan American Airways, he explains, needed at that time to run their airlines as quasi-official government bodies. McGregor's critics said that he ruled TCA as dictatorially as C.D. Howe had before him. It was also said that the former Battle of Britain pilot so loved all things British, that he bought the Vanguard airliner from his friend Sir George Edwards, at Vickers in England, before it could be properly tested. But when Gordon McGregor retired in 1968, Air Canada was one of the world's seven great airlines, on the cusp of the jumbo jet era. In his two decades as president, Canada's national airline had doubled in size every five years, and in 1968, employed 16,656 men and women. Even his detractors understood that for Air Canada, Gordon McGregor would be a tough act to follow. In 1980 when Claude Taylor was awarded the Royal Canadian Air Force Gordon McGregor Memorial Trophy, the award that must have renewed a few memories of his former boss.

McGregor had groomed Herb Seagrim, like himself a seasoned pilot, to take over the reins. But the days of cockpit presidents of airlines — giants like Grant McConachie, Howard Hughes and Eddie Rickenbaker had ended. Elected prime minister that year, Pierre Trudeau was made aware that the upper echelons of the government airline were almost exclusively English Canadian. Predictably, the national airline was attacked as an old boys club — and with many former RCAF officers and prewar TCA veterans still flying, there was some truth to this. The airline was a target that Trudeau's detractors both in Ottawa and Quebec City could not ignore. Consequently, McGregor was succeeded by Yves Pratte, a Quebec City lawyer who took the opportunity afforded all new chief excutives to immediately revamp the whole airline.

If the public perception of the airline at this time was as a bloated, inefficiently run Crown Corporation, it's employees were equally disenchanted. In 1969, the machinists' strike grounded the airline for thirty days even as Pratte brought in the McKinsey Company, an American firm of management consultants, to make recommendations on how Air Canada could turn a profit. By late 1973, the new 747s at $25 million apiece were bleeding the carefully hoarded surpluses from McGregors' administration dry. The problems multiplied; on the retirement of the Viscounts, the maintenance base at Winnipeg was closed, and this, together with the upheavals of bilingualism and labour problems, brought company morale to an all time low. But this was only the eye of the storm. The seventies also saw the original 1937 TCA family disappearing since many from the Lockheed Lodestar era took early retirement rather than work in the new environment. When Yves Menard, the first Air Canada French Canadian vice president resigned in 1975 in the face of a scandal, the airline seemed to be sinking like the *Titanic*. Through the summer of 1976, hearings were conducted on the management of the airline and allegations of conflict of interest were seldom out of the newspapers. Pratte, resigned on December 1, 1976, citing Ottawa's lack of support for his position and program of reorganisation.

By 1973, the new 747s at $25 million each, were bleeding the company's finances away.

Whoever accepted the job now, could have no illusions that there were wolves baying at the hangar doors. A lesser man than Claude Taylor might have refused. But in his twenty-seventh year with the airline, he accepted and was sworn in as president. He could not fly a Spitfire like McGregor but unlike Pratte he was not an outsider. He was well-liked for his enthusiasm, charming to the point of being famous for remembering everyone's children names and best of all, he had risen through the ranks. Taylor had trained as an accountant at McGill University's extension courses from 1950-53. He had been promoted steadily in the traffic administration department to become General Manager of Commercial Planning in 1962. He came to the attention of the company's director of operations, Dave Tennant, as early as 1957, by emphasizing sales strategy over mainly flying the flag.[2] Taylor was made Vice-President, Strategic Development in 1970 as the airline was undergoing some drastic changes. He had also been president of the Travel Industry Association and chairman of the Air Transport Association until 1976.

The new vice-president had already come to the attention of the Board of Directors due to his conduct of the bilateral negotiations for

---

2   Smith, Philip, *It Seems Like Only Yesterday*, Toronto: McClelland & Stewart, 1976, p. 37.

new routes into Europe, especially with his involvement in arranging the first flights to Moscow in 1966. In 1966, Taylor was sent to Moscow to negotiate with the Russian government. The thawing of the Cold War in the late 1960s and the heavy Russian involvement in EXPO 67 prompted the Canadian government to decide on an air link between the two countries. Unilateral détente was an initiative typical of Prime Minister Trudeau, one that he would repeat five years later with Beijing. There was a high level Soviet visit to Canada later that year and the prime minster was looking for something to sign. The agreement was taken off the shelf and signed amid historic handshakes on both sides.

In 1967, Air Canada DC-8s began flying to Moscow via Copenhagen since these jets did not have the range for nonstop flights. Contrary to popular opinion, the flights were not just symbolic gestures. As the only Western carrier to the Soviet Union, they did make money. There was little tourist traffic but the earliest cultural exchanges between North America and the USSR, and diplomatic travel from the United Nations in New York and the State Department in Washington filled the seats.

Now the president, Taylor's marketing experience warned him that the days of the state-subsidised airlines were coming to a close. But Air Canada then was still part of Canadian National Railways and received its policy directly from Ottawa. One of his priorities was to inform his managers, that from now on the airline was to be treated as a business and in the long term it would look to privatisation as the ultimate solution to it's problems. Fares had been kept artificially low and the new president had them raised to market level. Politicians in Ottawa claimed that nothing could be done until the CNR was itself privatised and no elected official wanted to be associated with that. It would take months of persuasion on Taylor's part but in 1977, Otto Lang, the Minister of Transport, tabled the Air Canada Act in the House of Commons. It came into effect on February 28 the following year, replacing the CNR with the federal government as the airline's owner and taking over its debt from the railway. Air Canada was now free to operate with a profit, to manage hotels, charter companies, and rent out its own expertise to other airlines — as its rival Canadian Pacific had done. It was no longer "the government's chosen intrument" as C.D. Howe saw it.

The airline began making money and paying dividends in the late 1970s. Removing the CNR mantle was a step in the right direction, its president thought, but it wasn't the whole journey by any means. Getting out from under the federal government's mantle and into the global market was the next logical step. But in 1978, before he could think about privatisation, the machinists went on strike that summer. The union staged rotating strikes and walk-outs across the country to the point that passengers began leaving Air Canada in droves. Taylor initially tried to plug the holes with clerical staff and warned that if the disruptions continued he would be forced to fire the strikers.

This caused the members to walk off the job, and he reluctantly grounded all aircraft on the morning of August 24, 1978. The strike was settled in ten days, opening a new era in labour relations between employees and management.

This was also the year that the deregulation of airlines began in the United States — a move that gradually spilled over into Canada. Now every airline would have access to all travel markets and Air Canada would no longer be protected from competition. CP Air (formerly Canadian Pacific Airlines) was allowed to fly transcontinental services and Wardair began taking a large segment of the charter market. Taylor was urged to downsize the workforce as a means of stemming off future deficit. But as long as Ottawa, specifically the Treasury Board and the Department of Transport held all the cards, Air Canada was hamstrung as a profit-making business. The growing debt also made it unattractive to suitors. Besides with the federal government always there to bail the company out, there was little incentive to improve its profitability.

Election years have always been ominous for Air Canada and in 1984, Brian Mulroney's campaign rhetoric had been that "Air Canada was not for sale." Taylor remembers telling Mulroney that the public would still vote for him if he promised to privatise Air Canada — that he (Taylor) had conditioned both the employees and the public on its viability. With the Conservative victory and a new Minister of Transport, Don Mazankowski, (who shared Taylor's vision), the climate for privatisation seemed clear but the prime minister's election statement about the airline's future delayed the momentum necessary for a quick sale. In December 1984, Taylor was hit by a car as he stepped off the curb at Dorchester and Peel streets in Montreal. Through the next year, as he recovered, and the government's bureaucracy laboriously cranked up to consider the sale of Air Canada.

One of outgoing Prime Minister Trudeau's last appointments was to make Pierre Jeanniot president and CEO of the airline, moving Taylor to the position of Chairman of the Board. Freed from his operating responsibilities, he could intensify his campaign for the privatisation, although in August 1986, his friend Don Mazankowksi was replaced at Transport Canada. Mr. Jeanniot was preoccupied with labour problems, his first challenges were negotiations to deal with the Canadian Auto Workers (CAW) and the Canadian Union of Public Employees (CUPE), which resulted in labour strikes but fortunately not a shut down of operations. The new CEO also began expanding the airline out of its traditional European/Caribbean territory to India and Singapore. The timing was unfortunate as the new routes lost money even as Air Canada started down the road to become a market-driven enterprise.

In February 1987, the list of companies to be privatised went to Cabinet for approval with Air Canada and Petro-Canada as the main contenders. The problem was that the airline had been given loans by banks on favourable terms precisely because it was backed by the government. The airline needed to upgrade to a fleet of fuel-efficient Airbuses costing about $3 billion. If the government backed out, so would the banks with their loans. Having come so far, Taylor would not accept partial privatisation. It took a torturous summer of negotiations for the banks to reach a settlement — just as the whole privatisation process in Britain came under critical review. "It looked like we got blown out of the water in October." Taylor recalled for *The Financial Times of Canada*.[3] "It looked like we had lost it. Suddenly everyone became very wise and said, that's why we didn't go ahead ..." The new year found him no closer to a solution.

Then Brian Mulroney reshuffled his Cabinet once more and Mazankowksi returned — this time as Deputy Prime Minister. Backed by such heavy artillery, Claude Taylor (who was adept at Commons hearings and committees), was able to push the deal through. A sure sign to him that the airline was on the block now was that no one at parties was talking to him about lost luggage anymore. Four years after Mulroney had said that the airline was not for sale, shares of it were offered to the public.

Ottawa had been encouraged by British Airways which launched a successful privatisation campaign in 1986 and already seemed to be

---

3   Anne Shortell, *Financial Times of Canada*, August 15, 1988, p. 12.

reaping the benefits of getting out from under the government's embrace. To raise cash and make the airline commercially viable, a series of reforms that ranged from selling off older aircraft to wage freezes and the downsizing of management positions was begun. These brought in a profit of $45.7 million, prompting the government to announce that 45% of the airlines shares would go on sale in September. The remaining 57% was put on the block in 1989. At $8.00 per share, the airline's employees were encouraged to "buy a piece of their employer," and 17,000 of the 23,000 employees did. The share values rose and fell as the airline industry reeled and recovered, reaching $14.88 in 1989 and plummeting to $2.20 in 1993. Many must have regretted their purchase, for the airline's losses were only made worse by the Gulf War. Jeanniot resigned in August 1990, citing lack of support for his reforms, and Claude Taylor once more became president and CEO, faced with pulling the airline out of turmoil again. He was now sixty-five years of age, a time when most men would be looking forward to retirement.

In the boom years of the 1960s, the federal government had divided Canada into regional markets for the smaller airlines like Nordair, Quebecair and Eastern Provincial Airways, restricting them to assigned routes and fares. When the National Transportation Act came into effect on January 1, 1988, both Canadian Airlines International and Air Canada jockeyed for position in the regional market by buying majority interests in local airlines like Nordair and charter airlines like Wardair. In this way the major airports could be linked with the smaller ones, the passenger ticketed all the way through from Toronto Island Airport to Tel Aviv. The regional market was a symptom of the intense competitiveness catalyzed by the levelling off of worldwide passenger growth and airline bankruptcy. By the start of the 1990s, recessions and deregulation were grounding airlines with frightening regularity. Wardair disappeared into Canadian Airlines International which then laid off 1,017 employees. What especially saddened Claude Taylor, and many in the airline profession, was the disappearance of an old friend like Pan American Airlines from the skies. It's death served as a constant reminder that either Air Canada or Canadian Airlines International could suffer the same fate.

Financial analysts estimated that by 1992 the airline was losing $1.2 million daily and Taylor and his board of directors cast around for partners to stop the hemorrhaging. Thousands of jobs had been

Taylor's decision to purchase smaller, fuel-efficient jets like this BAE-146 helped return the airline to profitability.

eliminated in 1990, and while Taylor was vilified by the trade unions and certain politicians, airline analysts blamed him for not getting rid of more people. Most of the airline's aircraft were now in need of replacement. The disastrous 1970s had prevented the airline from revamping its fleet and, by 1990, the 747s and DC-9s were getting long in the tooth — inefficient to run, impossible to fill. Coming on the market were the smaller, fuel-efficient BAE 146 and Bombardier mid-size jets, better suited for the cross-border destinations that were now opening up. Traditionally, airlines find the money to replace their fleets by trading in old aircraft. But just as Taylor opted to buy the new airliners to take advantage of "Open Skies" there was a glut of used aircraft on the market. Fortunately, every other airline in the world seemed to be cancelling orders and Air Canada could take advantage of the deep discounts and cheap loans to finance their younger fleet. Also in their favour was the excellent reputation of the workhorse DC-9s that made selling them off to the discount airlines easier.

Buying new aircraft was easy, Taylor used to say, but an airline's face was literally that of its employees — this was what the customer noticed. Air Canada's image was its flight attendants, counter staff, pilots and ground crew — not the Airbuses and 767s. He believed that every airline was dependent for its success on the culture that it had nurtured in its staff — Continental Airlines, Cathay Pacific and Singapore Airlines were good examples of that. It took a secure, loyal workforce that were enthusiastic about their jobs to bring the customers into those expensive, new aircraft. His rule of thumb for customer service onboard was; would you serve Claude Taylor that breakfast ?

Merging with Canadian Airlines International(CAI) would have been the logical choice for both money losers but CAI chose American Airlines as a partner instead. Taylor then offered to buy up CAI's international network, the routes that Grant McConachie had carved out for Canadian Pacific — Hong Kong, Thailand, Japan and Australia, now all profitable destinations. But they were part of CAI's dowry to American Airlines and were not about to be given up. He then put pressure on Ottawa to acquire the Pacific routes for Air Canada itself — especially the lucrative Hong Kong market, but he was stymied there too. He must have then reflected that there had been certain advantages to being the government's "chosen instrument".

Yet there was cause for some celebration. One cost saving measure was relocating the company's headquarters from the expensive Place Ville Marie complex in downtown Montreal to the maintenance base at Dorval. Marketing agreements with Swissair, United Airlines and Air France were signed. Other strategies included leasing aircraft out, and cutting 30 per cent of the workforce. These might have worked at any other time, but between 1990 and 1992, the whole airline industry was being devastated by market forces. The end result of his decisions was that Air Canada survived — bloodied and battered — but still in the air. By 1992, the corporate logos of Wardair, CP Air and Nationair were no longer seen at Canadian airports, but the familiar maple leaf of Air Canada had endured.

Critics muttered that Claude Taylor was too much a company man to eliminate the 10 per cent of the workforce necessary to compete in the private sector. It would take they said, someone more ruthless than the compassionate Maritimer — what one journalist called "a hired gun," to restructure a bloated former Crown corporation. The former reservations clerk was now sixty-seven years old and had held the line for sixteen years. Besides, he had many other outside interests — past president of the Boy Scouts, governor of local hospitals, universities and the Salvation Army and was an Officer of the Order of Canada and Member of the

Aviation Hall of Fame. He could take pride in his tenure as president, CEO and chairman of the board.

This time the airline's board of directors went outside Canada to hire a successor. In February 1992, Hollis Harris, former president of Delta Airlines and chairman of Continental Airlines began work at the Air Canada headquarters at Dorval. Claude Taylor was made chairman emeritus with responsibility for looking after the airline's investments in Continental Airlines. The view from his office window is of a sprawling Dorval Airport, where forty-two years ago, he got off a Lodestar from Moncton. He delights in reminding visitors that if they took TCA's whole airline fleet then and loaded it up with passengers, everyone would fit into a single 747.

Asked what he hoped his legacy would be, Claude Taylor replied that he hoped to be remembered for making enough of the right decisions during his tenure that allowed Air Canada to become the world-class airline it is today. He never achieved his boyhood ambition of becoming TCA's chief accountant in Winnipeg, but he had saved Canada's national airline. That is no mean feat.

JOHN ARMISTEAD WILSON
THE FATHER OF CIVIL AVIATION

Pearson, Dorval, Vancouver — today the big airports of Canada are cities in themselves, annually processing millions of passengers and employing thousands of skilled personnel. Despite the image of confusion that they often give, all are masterpieces of organisation, catering to passengers from the carpark to the departure lounge, responsible for their well-being even when their aircraft is a blip on the radar screen. How airports in Canada evolved from cow pastures to these mini-cites, indeed why they are where they are — for better or worse, is largely the work of a visionary Canadian that few know, J.A. Wilson.

John Armistead Wilson was born at Broughty Ferry, Scotland, on 2 November 1879. At sixteen, he was apprenticed to the engineering firm of James Carmichael & Sons at Dundee and later was trained as an engineer at St. Andrew's University. He went out to India in 1905 to seek his fortune and worked in Calcutta for Bird & Co. But because of ill health this ended abruptly and instead he emigrated to Canada. His first job was as an engineer for the Canada Cement Company, building plants at Exshaw, Alberta, and Hull, Quebec. Then in 1910, at the age of thirty-one, although he could not know it, his lifelong vocation in aviation began.

He accepted a position with the newly formed Department of Naval Service as its Director of Stores. Within nine years, Wilson had risen to the rank of Assistant Deputy Minister (ADM) of the Naval Service and was put in charge of the two Canadian naval air bases at Dartmouth and Sydney, Nova Scotia. While in the Service he became profoundly influenced by the complementary relationship between the Royal Navy and the merchant fleet. Each was indispensable to the other, as military and commercial aviation should be.

The first controller of aviation was the visionary, John Armistead Wilson who built airports across Canada.

PL117438

After the Armistice, the Naval Air Service was demobilised and the Air Board, a stop-gap measure was created by the government while it grappled with the strange new subject of aviation. Before the war, there existed no infrastructure, regulations or policy for this form of transport. Flying in 1913 was little more than an expensive way of committing suicide and aviators could barely get themselves airborne for a few minutes, let alone carry freight or passengers for a sustained flight. During the war, Canadian pilots at the Front were under the jurisdiction of British authorities. But in 1919, Ottawa was forced to come to terms with such concepts as airfields and formulating an aviation policy.

The postwar government of Prime Minister Robert Borden had no inclination to foster aviation, civil or military. A high level of unemployment combined with the six thousand veterans that needed hospitalisation left little money for subsidizing air companies or building airports. The prime minister stated that he was not about to waste urgently needed funds on a means of transport that benefited very few. To be fair to him, Canada had just come out of a war from which it had gained little and was still paying for the over-spending of the railway era.

For the public, aircraft were still a novelty. The biplanes of the day were seen as little more than expensive toys, used by barnstormers and unable to carry passengers en masse; they were no competition to the railways. For a nation that had supplied the Royal Flying Corps with almost half its pilots during the First World War, Canada quickly lost its lead in aviation through a lack of official enthusiasm. Wilson must have envied other nations and the practical uses that they had found for this new mode of transportation. In Europe, as the guns fell silent, the Royal Air Force was flying a passenger shuttle service between London and the Versailles Peace conference in Paris, and in 1924 Imperial Airways was designated Britain's chosen instrument i.e. the official airline. By 1920, there were five airlines operating in France and even defeated Germany had already launched Deutsche Luft Rederie with daily passenger service between Berlin and Weimar.

He helped draft the Air Board Act of 1919, the foundation of all laws dealing with aviation in Canada; even today it is considered a masterpiece of legislation. The Act established a Board of Aeronautics which had total control over all aviation in Canada, civil and military. It had three functions: regulation of civil aviation, aerial photography, forestry protection and as almost an afterthought, the aerial defence of the Dominion. On February 18, 1920, the government approved the Air Board's recommendations to form a non-permanent, non-professional Canadian Air Force. All former Royal Flying Corps airfields were put under the Air Board's jurisdiction and stocked with the war-surplus aircraft that had been given to Canada by the United States and Britain. By the Act, the federal government undertook the construction of a few airfields or seaplane bases like Jericho Beach, Vancouver and Rockliffe, Ottawa. The others were either former British bases like Camp Borden, Ontario, or those used for forestry patrols such as at Morley, Alberta. As one historian wrote, "No country ever spent less on civil aviation and no country has had greater returns for the money spent." It received Royal Assent on 6 June 1920, and Wilson resigned from his position in the Naval Service to become the Air Board's Secretary.

Three months later, the Air Board and Canadian Air Force sponsored a coast-to-coast flight across Canada. Not only would it publicize the Canadian Air Force but demonstrate that transcontinental airmail flights were possible. The historic flight began in high winds at Halifax harbour on October 7, 1920, and ended in Vancouver on the 17th. The pilots flew in relays, using first HS-2L and Felixstowe F.3 flying boats from Halifax to Winnipeg, fighting hurricane winds and engine trouble along the route. Hoping that they were setting a precedent, the pilots carried with them letters from the mayor of Halifax to his counterpart in Vancouver. When they landed in a rain storm on the Ottawa river before the nation's capital, Wilson was at the dock to greet them.

It was a journey comparable to that of the early explorers of the continent. If they crashed enroute there was little hope of being found, as once out of sight from the airfield, no one would know where they were.

From Winnipeg, two de Havilland 9A land planes completed the journey over the Rockies to Vancouver in poor weather. The bundle of letters sent by the mayor of Halifax had grown larger with every stop since at Winnipeg, Regina, Moose Jaw, Calgary, and Revelstoke, more official greetings were added[1]. When the last aircraft touched down on Sunday, 17 October on Richmond's rain-soaked racetrack in British Columbia, the letters had been flown 3,262 miles across Canada in 247 hours.

---

1   Frank Ellis, the country's foremost aviation historian tracked each set of letters down, and wrote in 1954 that all were preserved in the archives of the City of Vancouver.

With the first flight across Canada, Wilson had shown that given government support, transcontinental air mail was feasible. It was good public relations for both the Air Board and the Air Force.

Even then, Wilson knew that use of the Air Board's HS-2L seaplanes were limited to summer months, and although the country had lakes and rivers with frozen surfaces that could be used in the winter, a network of lighted, graded airports was a necessity.

Yet Parliament remained unconvinced. When it approved the Air Board's budget of $1.6 million, several Members voiced their opinions that it was a waste of money. In 1922, when Prime Minister Mackenzie King closed the Naval College and sold off most of the navy's ships, military officers within the Air Board must have realised that there was the serious likelihood of the Air Force going the same way. Sir Willoughby Gwatkin, its Director, understood that if it was to survive, the Air Force had to permanently establish itself — at the expense of Wilson's Air Board. On June 29, 1922, when the Department of National Defence came into being, the Air Board was disbanded and all aviation in Canada, civil and military was put under the jurisdiction of the Air Force.

A prolific writer, Wilson put his feelings into a letter to the deputy minister of defence on November 2nd, 1922. He demonstrated that the CAF, as part of the civil Air Board, had proven satisfactory and that there was no reason for discarding it without a public inquiry. There was also no legitimacy for the military to take over all of the Air Board's duties — government relations with commercial firms could never be adequately understood by Air Force officers. Rather than maintain Air Force bases, he wrote "... the Department of National Defence should aim at the strengthening of Aviation in all its phases. Air strength in Canada cannot depend on the Government's efforts alone but rest principally on the development of Commercial Aviation." He concluded that the government had not bothered to consult anyone who knew anything about the subject and that the control of commercial aviation was so obviously a civil matter that nothing more need be said.[2]

Wilson was aware that only the federal government had the resources to develop air transport across the vastness of Canada. He once astutely wrote that the problem with air companies in this country was that they

---

2   Public Archives of Canada, MG 30 E243, Vol 1.

were run by pilots and not businessmen. But few entrepreneurs would want to invest in Canadian air companies when the odds were so daunting. It wasn't only that the climate was inhospitable, but in the second decade of this century, most of northern Canada had barely been surveyed. The country's early explorers had relied on water routes that ran east and west and, other than its coastline, little was known of the north.

In order to map the country, Canada first needed to be surveyed and photographed. In 1923 when he became the Civil Aviation Secretary in the new Department of Defence, Wilson made aerial observation its first priority. He was fortunate that in the euphoria of a world thought to be forever at peace, the Air Force was envisioned less as airborne warriors than as a cadre of military pilots engaged in civil duties like forest fire patrols, fisheries protection, treaty money distribution and aeronautical experimentation. These duties were performed at the expense of commercial aviation, but they gave the Air Force a raison d'être in difficult times, at minimum expense.

Then on July 1, 1927, without consulting Wilson, the new Liberal government reorganised the Department of National Defence. The DND was now given overall responsibility for military and civil aviation and he was made Controller of Civil Aviation; (he later said that there was precious little to control). His view that the Air Force's existence should be based on "economic development for peace uses" was well known and must have made him unpopular with the military.

But "J.A." (as Wilson liked to be called) will always be remembered for the building of the Trans-Canada Airway — a series of government airfields from coast-to-coast, about 100 miles apart, that would allow safe and efficient air travel along a trunk route. On November 25, 1929, he set out his plan for developing a Trans-Canada air route.

"Canada is one of the great trading countries of the world. Our trans-Atlantic and trans-Pacific commerce is vital to us. We occupy the most favourable position geographically to both. Already airship services are being experimented with, seadrome routes are being considered linking all continents and the trans-Arctic airway is mooted. All these matters are of immense importance not only politically but commercially. The close association of the great railway systems with our aviation would strengthen it enormously and bring to it a wider outlook and influence in transportation and its organisation, domestic and worldwide."[3]

To help his vision succeed, he was fortunate to have General A.G.L. McNaughton as an ally. McNaughton served as Chief of the General Staff from 1929 to 1935 and although primarily concerned with defence, saw that a network of airstrips across the country could have military as well as civil benefits. On February 22, 1929, Order in Council PC 322 authorised the Department of National Defence to begin contributing towards the building of the Trans-Canada Airway.

Wilson travelled across the country extensively, choosing sites for airfields, power lines and radio beacons, using road, rail and sometimes rail car to get deep into the bush. Because of the terrain, the airfields on the prairies were the easiest to construct and were completed by 1929. This allowed Western Canada Airways to fly the mail from Winnipeg to Edmonton on a schedule, and at night. By 1930, one could travel by air from Moncton, New Brunswick to Edmonton, Alberta refuelling on airfields of the Airway, flying clubs and municipal airports. Unfortunately, between Toronto and Winnipeg, it meant going south of the border to Detroit, on the American airlines to North Dakota, then recrossing the Manitoba border.

The massive unemployment caused by the Depression proved a blessing in disguise for both Wilson and McNaughton. Relief measures for the unemployed were now beyond the capacity of the local governments to alleviate. Relief camps were set up by the Department of National Defence for the thousands of homeless, unemployed men, and McNaughton was put in charge of administrating them in a make work scheme. The men were transported by the military, fed military rations, and were free to leave if unsatisfied with the conditions. The Trans-Canada Airway was ideal for this; it took work away from no one and, because it was so labour-intensive, apart from wheelbarrows, handtools and dynamite, little in the way of construction machinery was needed.

Transported into the bush, the relief workers drained, cleared and levelled sites for landing strips at 100 mile intervals across Canada. At its height in 1933, over 10,000 men were employed at forty-six sites; they

---

3   J.A. Wilson, *The Development of Aviation in Canada* 1879-1948, Ottawa: The King's Printer, 1950, p.14.

were housed, clothed and fed, and paid a maximum of one dollar per day. The relief scheme did have its critics who claimed that it was designed to take potential recruits for radical movements and labour activists out of the cities and isolate them in the bush.

Wilson travelled the length of the Airway ceaselessly, constantly checking its progress, his training as an engineer now being put to good use. The most difficult section was in northern Ontario between Cochrane and Kenora. By 1931, Calgary, Saskatoon and Lethbridge were added to the prairie route. Although the Trans-Canada Airway was not officially open, on 28 September, 1935, Wilson was the first person to fly it from Ottawa and Winnipeg, as a passenger in a Stearman biplane. In November 1936, urban municipalities that couldn't afford to build airports or improve on their present sites were given a government grant to do so and several of the mammoth airports today owe their beginnings to this policy.

When Mackenzie King's Liberals returned to power that year, they inaugurated the most air-minded era in Canadian history. The formation of the Department of Transport (DOT) on November 1, 1936, divorced military and civil aviation forever. The RCAF was relieved of its civil duties and made to concentrate on home defence. Besides founding Trans-Canada Air Lines, C.D. Howe, the new Minister for Transport, also pushed the Transport Act through Parliament. Wilson was made a director of Trans-Canada Air Lines in 1937 and accompanied Howe in the famous dawn-to-dusk cross-country flight. Civil aviation's new strength was further increased by the appointment of a Board of Transport Commissioners who handled such duties as the licensing of air routes and tariffs.

On September 1, 1938, Wilson made an inspection tour of the airports on the Airway, flying from Toronto to Vancouver, and then north with the ubiquitous Grant McConachie of United Air Transport to Whitehorse in the Yukon. It had taken almost a decade, but the Trans-Canada Airway was completed. Overshadowed almost immediately by the Second World War, the chain of fully equipped airports and radio beacon stations across the continent has never received the attention it deserved, but it changed the economic and social face of our country forever. The airports not only made airmail and later passenger service between the cities possible, but the large ones like Toronto's Malton Airport became economic generators and during the war, military bases.

But Wilson was already looking beyond Canada to trans-Atlantic flight. As early as 1932, he wrote to a British friend that "while the past few years had seen a build up of a system of air communications on the different continents, with the increasing efficiency of aircraft, men's minds would naturally turn towards international services as the next logical step. The Atlantic crossing was by far the most important trade route in the world ... and on it if anywhere, will be found traffic sufficient in volume and value to justify the addition of an air service to the transportation facilities now serving the needs of its trade and commerce."[4] But his optimism could not take into account the Second World War when all Atlantic air travel was restricted to military purposes.

Early in the conflict, a joint agreement for large scale air crew training was signed by Canada, Britain, Australia and New Zealand. The Civil Aviation Division of the Department of Transport was given the responsibility for the survey and selection of the airfields needed. With experience gained by the airfield building program, he took on much of the work personally. Although the agreement to form the British Commonwealth Air Training Plan (BCTAP) was signed on 17 December 1939, (Mackenzie King's birthday), early that autumn, Wilson and his inspectors had already been busy mapping out possible sites and planning the construction of airfields. His organising ability combined with his personal knowledge of the terrain helped create 148 new airports in a record time. After the flying training schools were completed in 1942, Howe sent Wilson to London to make arrangements to negotiate the Canadian Government Trans-Atlantic Air Service (CGTAS).

"J.A." retired from the DOT on July 18, 1945, with many honours. He was awarded the Trans-Canada (McKee) Trophy, created a Commander of the Order of the British Empire, and given the Norwegian Medal for Freedom. As a keen aviation historian, he officiated at several airport openings and attended flying club conventions. Many of his civil air regulations remain in use today. He died at Ottawa on October 10, 1954, just as the jet age was about to change his airports drastically. Of all the honours he received, being remembered as the "Father of Civil Aviation in Canada" would have meant the most to him.

---

4   J.A. Wilson "Internationalism of Civil Aviation" 1932, Dhist. Wilson papers, folder BB.